Justice-Home Affairs Diplomacy

The Palermo Treaty System in the New Era

nova science publishers
www.novapublishers.com

Law, Crime and Law Enforcement

More information about this series can be found at
https://novapublishers.com/product-category/series/law-crime-and-law-enforcement/

Laws and Legislation

More information about this series can be found at
https://novapublishers.com/product-category/series/laws-and-legislation-series/

Anis H. Bajrektarevic
Carlos López-Veraza Pérez

Justice-Home Affairs Diplomacy

The Palermo Treaty System in the New Era

nova
science publishers
www.novapublishers.com

DOI: https://doi.org/10.52305/MKCV6537

Library of Congress Cataloging-in-Publication Data

ISBN: 979-8-89530-656-7 (Softcover)
ISBN: 979-8-89530-809-7 (eBook)

Published by Nova Science Publishers, Inc. † New York

Contents

Chapter 1

Towards Universal Justice in the Fight against Transnational Crime

The current decade has been marked by significant turbulence, bringing profound changes and challenges at many levels. After the pandemic, tragic events have taken place that are threatening the foundations of global security. These include a rise in armed conflicts, territorial challenges, and severe attacks on human rights. All this is happening at a time when we may be facing the greatest revolution since the emergence of digital technologies, or even since the Industrial Revolution. Scholars and international agencies have warned of the significant risks that the use of artificial intelligence could pose to global security[1]. As AI technologies advance, concerns grow about their potential misuse in creating deep fakes, automating cyberattacks, and orchestrating sophisticated phishing schemes, necessitating vigilant international regulatory measures.

Globalization has not only transformed the way we do business and communicate, but has also enabled complex global criminal dynamics that transcend national borders. One of these challenges is transnational crime. As globalization advances, the borders that historically defined sovereign limits are becoming less relevant for criminal organizations, creating ideal conditions for the emergence and expansion of illicit activities that operate beyond national jurisdictions.

The nature of transnational crime has changed significantly in recent years. Traditional crimes, such as drug trafficking, corruption, and terrorism-related activities, pose major global risks.

Cybercrime, for example, has accelerated dramatically in recent years - criminal networks and hackers now target not only individuals and businesses but also key infrastructure and government institutions worldwide. Furthermore, the rise of blockchain-based assets has led to new forms of

---

[1] National Institute of Standards and Technology. *Artificial Intelligence Risk Management Framework*. U.S. Department of Commerce, January 2023. Accessed November 24, 2024. https://doi.org/10.6028/NIST.AI.100-1.

money laundering, making it more challenging to track, pursue, and recover laundered money.

At the same time, other major threats - like human trafficking, environmental crime, and terrorist financing - have also evolved, driven by increased global mobility and rapid technological advances. This underscores the urgent need for robust international cooperation and adaptive legal frameworks capable of keeping pace with the evolving nature of transnational crime.

There is also a rise in environmental crimes, including the illegal wildlife trade and deforestation. In this context, criminal networks are using new technologies, making it harder for law enforcement to track and disrupt their operations.

This not only makes it harder to investigate and prosecute these crimes because they can operate across borders easily, but also poses serious threats to states. These activities undermine trust in institutions, fuel corruption, and can infiltrate legitimate parts of the economy and political systems, making them especially dangerous. In some parts of the world - so-called "black spots" where the rule of law is fragile or compromised - these groups operate with almost total impunity. They have even been referred to as new versions of pirate islands[2], highlighting the need for a coordinated global fight to confront them effectively. Given the cross-border nature of transnational crime, state-level responses are insufficient without multilateral engagement, and it is therefore essential that progress be made on the system established by the United Nations Convention against Transnational Organized Crime (hereinafter, Palermo Convention or UNTOC[3]) and Protocols thereto and other multilateral conventions, such as the Convention against Corruption (hereinafter, UNCAC or Mérida Convention)[4]. The lines between transnational organized crime, terrorism, trafficking in persons, and corruption are often blurred, creating a complex web of interconnected threats that require a comprehensive and coordinated response. The digital revolution has profoundly impacted transnational organized crime, providing new tools for communication, financial transactions, and the distribution of illicit goods and services.

---

[2] Stuart S. Brown and Margaret G. Hermann. *Transnational Crime and Black Spots: Rethinking Sovereignty and the Global Economy*. Cham: Palgrave Macmillan, 2020.

[3] United Nations General Assembly. United Nations Convention against Transnational Organized Crime. A/RES/55/25 (January 8, 2001).

[4] United Nations General Assembly. United Nations Convention against Corruption. A/58/422 (October 31, 2003).

A multidimensional international strategy - centered on asset recovery, corporate accountability, and judicial cooperation - is essential to address these emerging threats.

1.1. Concept of Organized Crime

Transnational organized crime takes the concept of organized crime a step further, transcending national borders and jurisdictions. It involves criminal enterprises that operate on a global scale, exploiting the interconnectedness of our modern world. These criminal networks use technology, trade, and communication to facilitate their illicit activities across multiple countries. Transnational organized crime has become a formidable challenge due to globalization and the use of new technologies.

Although organized crime has been visible in Europe for decades, it attracted very little attention at high political and economic levels in Europe in the last years of the 20th century. Simultaneously, the radical changes in Central and Eastern European Countries of the late 1980s implied growing possibilities for organized crime to carry out transboundary operations throughout Europe. Consequently, the criminal markets have become increasingly mobile, adaptable, and highly profitable. Hence, the problem has gained visibility in recent years, and international cooperation has advanced to fight new forms of organized crime.

The Palermo Convention does not define transnational organized crime, but it provides the characteristics that should characterize every organized criminal group. According to Article 2 of the Palermo Convention, it must consist of three or more persons who were not randomly formed; exist for a period of time; act in concert with the aim of committing at least one offense punishable by imprisonment of at least four years; and exist to obtain, directly or indirectly, a financial or other material benefit.

For their part, the European Commission and the Council of Europe's Expert Group on Organized Crime[5] have been considering that a series of requirements must be met such as: (i) a collaboration of three or more persons; (ii) a prolonged or indefinite period; (iii) participants suspected or convicted

---

[5] Francesco Calderoni. *Organized Crime Legislation in the European Union: Harmonization and Approximation of Criminal Law, National Legislations and the EU Framework Decision on the Fight Against Organized Crime*. Milan: Università Cattolica del Sacro Cuore, 2010.

of committing serious criminal offenses; (iv) the objective of pursuing profit and/or power.

Among the optional criteria (eventually) are: (v) having a specific task or role for each participant; (vi) using a form of internal discipline and control; (vii) using violence or other means suitable for intimidation; (viii) exerting influence on politics, the media, public administration, law enforcement, the administration of justice or the economy by corruption or using other means; (ix) using commercial or business-like structures; (x) engagement in money laundering; and (xi) operating on an international level.

The UN 1994 Naples Political Declaration and Global Action Plan against Organized Transnational Crime[6] specified the following six characteristics of organized crime, which might be transnational: (i) there has to be a group organized to commit crime; (ii) hierarchical links or personal relations which enable leaders to control the group; (iii) the use of violence, intimidation and corruption to earn profits or control territories or markets; (iv) the laundering of illicit proceeds to further criminal activity and to infiltrate the legitimate economy; (v) a potential for expansion into any new activity beyond national borders; and finally (vi) co-operation with other organized transnational criminal groups.

These characteristics highlight how difficult it is to combat transnational organized crime in a globalized world and emphasize the need for concerted international collaboration.

1.2. International Regime

As the world becomes more connected, organized crime has adapted and gained a new dimension. Transnational criminal groups do not act in one country - they move across borders, using the global flow of people, money, and technology to run their operations.

This kind of crime is a real threat and puts states at risk. That is why the global community is building a system - made up of treaties, agreements, and shared tools - to fight organized crime as one. It is an ongoing effort to make sure countries are not fighting this battle alone, but standing together to stop these networks of crime, bring criminals to justice, and protect people everywhere.

---

[6] UN General Assembly. *Naples Political Declaration and Global Action Plan against Organized Transnational Crime.* A/RES/49/159 *(February 24, 1995).*

The last few decades have marked a significant breakthrough in the efforts towards the international regime against transnational crime and a more structured and interlinked set of rules and provisions of international law has been developed (often pre-supposing the advanced development of both institutions and instruments). Therefore, we can safely say that by now these instruments are creating a (new) practice of states, which theory usually labels as "The International Regime". Among the essential instruments, some of the fundamental ones are brokered at the Office on Drugs and Crime[7] (UNODC) - a Vienna based part of the UN Secretariat that primarily deals with crimes and (narcotic) drugs, including corruption and a small branch department on terrorism prevention (TPB). It operates in 98 countries, with 2500 UNODC personnel globally[8]. The UNODC is a guardian of the Narcotic Drugs Treaty System[9] as well as the Organized Crime - Corruption Treaty System.

Since dealing with the problems of crime and narcotic drugs confronts us with clandestine, illicit and nearly always illegal trans-border criminal activity, we have, first of all, to make an important distinction between two legal terms: (I) international crime and (ii) transnational crime:

(i) the former refers to offenses prescribed by international law, which can be prosecuted (previously by the international tribunals, including the Ad Hoc tribunals for the former Yugoslavia as well as for Rwanda, and now, by the standing International Criminal Court, as the Rome Statute[10] which entered into force in July 2002.

(ii) Transnational crime rather refers to more conventional (nationally proscribed) crimes which do involve more than one national jurisdiction, and therefore require a transnational and/or cross- border response.

When dealing with issues of transnational crime, the usual response is a treaty or (multilateral/trilateral, bilateral) agreement between the state parties as to ensure that:

---

[7] United Nations Office on Drugs and Crime, "Office on Drugs and Crime," accessed November 22, 2024, https://www.unodc.org/.

[8]United Nations Office on Drugs and Crime. "UNODC Field Offices." Accessed October 24, 2024. https://www.unodc.org/unodc/en/field-offices.html.

[9] United Nations. *Single Convention on Narcotic Drugs (1961); Convention on Psychotropic Substances (1971); and Convention against Illicit Traffic in Narcotic Drugs and Psychotropic Substances (1988).*

[10] United Nations General Assembly. *Rome Statute of the International Criminal Court.* Adopted July 17, 1998.

- the very conduct involved is a crime proscribed by domestic law;
- each state party has adequate jurisdiction to investigate, prosecute and punish offenses which occur only partly on their territory or which have other links, such as the involvement of citizens as either offenders or victims;
- state parties agree to provide necessary forms of cooperation to each other.

These are the basic functions of the multilateral legal instruments such as the Palermo Convention and the UN Convention against Corruption.

As transnational organized crime grows, becomes more sophisticated, and proliferates, there is an evident need to expand the existing body of international legislation. These requests are not without controversies, as the experience with the International Criminal Court illustrates:

- it is still understood that international treaties cause certain erosion of national sovereignty and that they do hinder domestic political priorities for crime-control;
- treaties are expensive to administer and moderately effective in the monitoring of compliance mechanisms;
- finally, treaties are usually negotiated on consensus, which ensures broad basis for agreement, but a "lowest common denominator" on substance – the provisions are what everyone could agree upon and often do not go as far as some state parties would like (or have incorporated into in their own legislation).

However, the international criminal law treaties will almost certainly be expanded as pressures to deal with global problems are gradually overcoming national reluctance. Consequently, it was expected that new instruments would be adopted against varied sorts of transnational organized crime in the form of additional protocols to the Palermo Convention. Despite this, more than 20 years have passed, and it does not look like it will be extended for the time being. However, this does not prevent the UNTOC from adapting to new forms of organized crime. It is a flexible legal instrument, drafted in broad terms, so that it can adapt to the times. After addressing narcotic drugs, organized crime, terrorism financing, and corruption through various treaties, the international community is now turning its attention to crimes involving the private or corporate sector and of individual or non-organized crime.

1.3. Multilateral Efforts in Fighting Organized Crime

Activities on a supranational and intergovernmental level to combat organized crime have existed since 1923 (Interpol). Present international/regional fora trying to combat transnational organized crime and to improve criminal justice are the European Union/Commission, EUROPOL, Council of Europe; as well as the global/universal ones: Interpol–ICPO and UNODC, formerly ODCCP (CICP and DCP).

1.3.1. European Union

Before the Maastricht Treaty[11] there was no specific EU–framework for dealing with matters related to organized crime (only informal police co-operation between member states, initiated in the mid-1970s, which was gradually expanded to deal with organized crime – among others in the context of the TREVI group).

The Maastricht Treaty made specific provisions in the field of Justice and Home Affairs (hereinafter, JHA), leading to the establishment of a formal co-operation structure for customs and police matters, as well as for criminal and judicial issues. Within the framework of this structure, working groups on police co-operation, drugs and organized crime, corruption, money-laundering, terrorism, and judicial co-operation were established.

A Pre-accession Pact (resting upon the Copenhagen accession criteria of 1993[12]) on organized crime between the EU member states and the EU candidate countries was approved as early as 1998 (after the Amsterdam and shortly before the Nice Treaty). The main purpose of this Pact was to develop a joint annual strategy to identify the most significant measures against organized crime (including a two-way flow of information, the exchange of liaison officers, joint investigative activities and special operations carried out with Europol's support).

---

[11]European Union. *Treaty on European Union (Consolidated Version), Treaty of Maastricht.* Official Journal of the European Communities C 325/5 (February 7, 1992).

[12] Christophe Hillion. "Enlarging the European Union and Deepening Its Fundamental Rights Protection." *Swedish Institute for European Policy Studies* (June 2013): 2.

Since the Maastricht Treaty, and especially since the provisions of the Amsterdam (and Nice) Treaty[13] entered into force at a special JHA meeting of the European Council with the EU Heads of State or Government in Tampere, Finland in October 1999 (also the Seville European Council of June 2002), the European Union has further strengthened its structures as well as its cross- EU and pan-European cooperation.

Following the meeting held in Tampere in 1999, it was stipulated that a judicial body for judicial cooperation comprising judges, prosecutors, and police should be set up. Further incentives were brought about at the EU Council summit in Nice, France, on 09th of December 2000 as it agreed to establish Eurojust[14]. Since then, Eurojust has grown steadily, culminating in the Treaty of Lisbon[15], which specifically established its function of support and cooperation between national authorities in cases of serious crimes affecting two or more member states· In December 2019, Eurojust became the EU Agency for Criminal Cooperation, and a new regulation entered into force.

After the entry into force of the Lisbon Treaty, security became a shared competence between the European Union and the member states.

Furthermore, the European Union established in 2010 a four-year policy cycle to address the European Union's main threats[16] (European Multidisciplinary Platform Against Criminal Threats, EMPACT). The European Council defines in each cycle what the priorities are, considering recommendations from other agencies, such as Frontex or Eurojust. In the EMPACT programs, particular emphasis is put on crimes such as migrant smuggling, child abuse, environmental crimes, cybercrime, document fraud, money laundering, drug trafficking, and arms trafficking[17].

The proposal by the European Commission for a European strategy against organized crime stresses the need to promote international cooperation, break down the structures of international organizations and their

---

[13] Treaty of Nice, art. 31: "The Council shall promote cooperation through EUROJUST by promoting support for criminal investigations in cases of serious cross-border crime, particularly organized crime, taking into account analyses carried out by Europol."

[14] European Union Agency for Criminal Justice Cooperation. "History." Accessed November 14, 2024. https://www.eurojust.europa.eu/about-us/history.

[15] European Union Treaty of Lisbon Amending the Treaty on European Union and the Treaty Establishing the European Community. 2007/C 306/01. December 13, 2007.

[16] Europol. "EU Policy Cycle." Accessed November 14, 2024. https://www.europol.europa.eu/crime-areas-and-statistics/empact.

[17] Katrien Luyten and Sofija Voronova, "Understanding the EU Response to Organised Crime," *European Parliamentary Research Service*, accessed November 14, 2024, published September 2020, https://www.europarl.europa.eu/RegData/etudes/BRIE/2020/652043/EPRS_BRI

methods of infiltrating economies, and combat the use of new technologies by criminals[18].

In 2016, in an unprecedented development in criminal cooperation in the European Union, the member states of the European Union agreed on the creation of a European Public Prosecutor's Office[19], with power to investigate fraud, corruption, money laundering, and cross-border VAT fraud.

1.3.2. Europol

The Maastricht Treaty and other EU regulations created the opportunity for wider police co-operation in the field of combating (transnational) organized crime – something that has been reaffirmed in the Reform/Lisbon Treaty of 2007[20].

EDU (European Drug Unit), a first step towards the establishment of Europol, was established by the decision of the European Council in 1993[21]. EDU was mandated to cover: (i) illicit drugs trafficking; (ii) immigration networking; (iii) theft-vehicle trafficking, and finally in 1996, EDU got an additional mandate to cover (iv) trafficking in persons. The Europol Convention entered into force on 01 October 1998, mandating this agency to follow illegal/illicit trafficking in nuclear and radioactive substances; in persons, vehicles, and drugs, as well as the money laundering related to it. Since January 1999, Europol is additionally charged to cover terrorism, cybercrime, and child pornography (eventually through SIRENE system[22]). Over the past 20 years, Europol has carried out thousands of investigations against criminal organizations with international activities. These have included remarkable international operations against drug trafficking, terrorism, cybercrime, counterfeiting, facilitation of illegal immigration,

---

[18] European Union, *Communication from the Commission on the EU Strategy to Tackle Organised Crime 2021–2025* (Brussels, April 14, 2021).

[19] European Union, Council Regulation (EU) 2017/1939 of 12 October 2017 Implementing Enhanced Cooperation on the Establishment of the European Public Prosecutor's Office ('the EPPO'), Official Journal of the European Union L 283 (October 31, 2017): 1–71.

[20] European Union, Treaty of Lisbon Amending the Treaty on European Union and the Treaty Establishing the European Community (December 13, 2007).

[21] European Union, Council Decision of 6 April 2009 Establishing the European Police Office (Europol), Official Journal of the European Union L 121 (May 15, 2009): 37–66.

[22] European Commission, "Information on SIRENE Cooperation," accessed November 24, 2024, https://home-affairs.ec.europa.eu/policies/schengen-borders-and-visa/schengen-information-system/sirene-cooperation_fr.

corruption, or child sexual exploitation[23] Finally, Europol cooperates with countries outside the European Union and international organizations such as the Council of Europe, UN, and other relevant fora.[24]

1.3.3. Council of Europe

The Council of Europe, as the single pan-European forum, has its own intergovernmental work program against crime that is channeled through the European Committee on Crime Problems[25] (CDPC). It strengthened the cooperation between member states in combating organized crime.

Among the major outcomes of this "principal legislative machinery of Europe" (which since 1945 has brokered over 200 conventions and treaties[26]), the Council of Europe adopted the Convention on Cybercrime, 2001[27] and the Additional Protocol to the Convention on Cybercrime in 2002 (111th Session of the Committee of Ministers of the Council of Europe),[28] the Trafficking in Human Beings Convention in 2005[29] and the Convention on the Prevention of Terrorism in 2006[30]. For the past decade, the Council of Europe has continued its legislative line and adopted new conventions to prevent and combat transnational crimes: in 2011, the Convention on preventing and combating violence against women and domestic violence[31] (it also addresses human trafficking and forced marriages affecting women) and the Convention on the Counterfeiting of Medical Products and similar crimes involving threats to

---

[23] Europol, "Europol's Most Noteworthy Operations," accessed December 16, 2024, https://www.europol.europa.eu/about-europol/europol-20-years/europols-20-most-noteworthy-operations.

[24] Europol, "Strategic Agreements," accessed November 24, 2024, https://www.europol.europa.eu/partners-agreements/strategic-agreements.

[25] Council of Europe, "European Committee on Crime Problems," accessed November 14, 2024, https://www.coe.int/en/web/cdpc/home.

[26] Council of Europe, "Treaty Office," accessed November 14, 2024, https://www.coe.int/en/web/conventions.

[27] Council of Europe, Convention on Cybercrime, CETS No. 185 (Budapest, November 23, 2001).

[28] Council of Europe, Explanatory Report to the Convention on Cybercrime, CETS No. 185 (Budapest, November 23, 2001).

[29] Council of Europe, Council of Europe Convention on Action Against Trafficking in Human Beings, CETS No. 197 (Warsaw, May 16, 2005).

[30] Council of Europe, Convention on the Prevention of Terrorism, CETS No. 196 (Warsaw, May 16, 2005).

[31] Council of Europe, Convention on Preventing and Combating Violence Against Women and Domestic Violence, CETS No. 210 (Istanbul, May 11, 2011).

public health[32] (the Medicrime Convention); in 2015, the Convention against Trafficking in Human Organs[33] and in 2017 the Council of Europe Convention on Offenses relating to Cultural Property [34](in the framework of the terrorism and organized crime). On September 5, 2024, the Council of Europe adopted the Convention on Artificial Intelligence and Human Rights, Democracy, and the Rule of Law, the first legally binding international instrument on artificial intelligence[35].

1.3.4. Interpol – (ICPO-International Criminal Police Organization)

Interpol enjoys a membership of 196 countries[36] and a world-wide telecommunication network which links each member's National Crime Bureau (NCB) by Interpol's secure internal communication network (I-mail), and gives automated access to centralized database (and the basic background information) on international crime and criminal gangs. The NCBs are (as an exchange mechanism) a key element in the services Interpol provides to its member countries. The NCB serves as a link between law enforcement agencies of one country and the law enforcement agencies of other member countries. The growth and threat of criminal organizations has been elaborated in various resolutions and other deliberations adopted by the Interpol General Assembly (GA) sessions[37] during the '70s and '80s. The use of encryption, dark web markets, and cryptocurrency transactions allows criminal organizations to operate with greater anonymity and evade detection, making it increasingly difficult for law enforcement to track their activities.

By the Interpol GA Resolution[38], a working group on organized crime was created in 1988. This resolution noted that "...organized crime does not limit itself to one form of criminal activity." As a result of this resolution Interpol

---

[32] Council of Europe, Convention on the Counterfeiting of Medical Products and Similar Crimes Involving Threats to Public Health, CETS No. 211 (Moscow, October 28, 2011).

[33] Council of Europe, Convention Against Trafficking in Human Organs, CETS No. 216 (Santiago de Compostela, March 25, 2015).

[34] Council of Europe: Committee of Ministers, Framework Convention on Offenses Relating to Cultural Property, CETS No. 221 (May 3, 2017).

[35] Council of Europe, Convention on Artificial Intelligence and Human Rights, Democracy and the Rule of Law, CETS No. 225 (Vilnius, September 5, 2024).

[36]Interpol, "Information on Interpol Member Countries," accessed November 24, 2024, https://www.interpol.int/Who-we-are/Member-countries.

[37] Interpol, "Resources and Documentation," accessed November 14, 2024, https://www.interpol.int/Resources/Documents.

[38] Interpol, Organized Crime, Resolution No. AGN/57/RES/17 (1988).

later created the Organized Crime Branch at the General Secretariat in 1989[39]. A subsequent Resolution adopted at the 1993 General Assembly further emphasized the need for international co-operation in combating organized crime[40], by recommending that "the ICPO-Interpol should continue to encourage police efforts and to intensify co-operation between countries and their police services, ...seeking to improve the exchange of information between countries, and analysis of that information, and to promote participation by all countries in the structure created within the ICPO-Interpol to deal with this subject." The long-term aim of the Organized Crime Branch was to create an extensive and comprehensive data base of organized criminal enterprises and persons who are engaged in continued, illegal activity to generate (illicit) profits.

The Organized Crime Branch realized that organized crime groups were increasingly active in migrant smuggling and trafficking of human beings. Therefore, in 1996, Project 'Marco Polo' was initiated to produce a study on the routes, modus operandi and organized crime groups involved in irregular migrations from any country to Western Europe.

The Marco Polo study[41], published in 1997, clearly showed that the largest number of non- European illegal immigrants coming to Western Europe between 1992 and 1997 had originated from either Iraq, Sri Lanka, Pakistan, India, or one of the African countries (such as Nigeria, Rwanda, or Somalia). Several routes utilized in the smuggling of Chinese nationals to Western Europe were also noted in the Marco Polo study. The Organized Crime Branch collects and analyses several other, but equally important cases of illegal immigration and trafficking in human beings[42]. Upon evaluation, Interpol intends to send its specialized officers and analysts to assist local police units during the ongoing investigations (which are of relevance at the international level).

The current intention of Interpol is to provide its member countries with a better insight into the linkage between organized crime groups, on the one hand, and the illegal immigration and trafficking in human beings on the other hand (description of groups, their membership, ordinary routes, methods and

---

39 Interpol. "Key Dates." Accessed November 24, 2024. https://www.interpol.int/Who-we-are/Our-history/Key-dates.

40 Interpol. "Key Dates."

41 International Centre for Migration Policy Development, *The Relationship Between Organised Crime and Trafficking in Aliens* (Vienna: ICMPD, 2010), 10.

42 Interpol, "Human Trafficking and Migrant Smuggling," accessed December 10, 2024, https://www.interpol.int/Crimes/Human-trafficking-and-migrant-smuggling.

means of transportation, location of safe houses, identity of escorts, suppliers of forged documents, as well as visa fraud methods). Special emphasis will be put on the collection and dissemination of information related to the post-smuggling/trafficking networking of organized crime groups (involving trafficked persons into activities such as: forced labor, organized begging, pick-pocketing, prostitution, pornography, terrorism, etc.).

As for refocusing attention on the public and private sector, the ICPO organized several international meetings, bringing together experts, public and private organizations from all over the world on issues such as the fight against terrorism and human trafficking[43]. In recent years, Interpol has focused its work on the need to recover the proceeds of crime, fight corruption[44] that diminishes trust in governments and institutions, cooperate actively with the private sector and break the business model of criminal organizations[45].

1.3.5. United Nations

The United Nations and its Vienna-based Office for Drugs and Crimes, formerly ODCCP; including the Drug Control Program – UNDCP, and the Centre for International Crime Prevention and Criminal Justice – CICP, play a significant global role in combating organized crime and in strengthening criminal justice[46].

The first important step, regarding the relevant United Nations activities, was the 1988 UN Convention against Illicit Traffic in Narcotic Drugs and Psychotropic Substances[47] which contains provisions requiring the development of international co-operation in the fields of extradition, asset

---

[43] Interpol, "5th Interpol Global Conference on Trafficking in Human Beings and Smuggling of Migrants," accessed November 24, 2024, https://www.interpol.int/fr/Actualites-et-evenements/Evenements/2017/5th-INTERPOL-Global-Conference-on-Trafficking-in-Human-Beings-and-Smuggling-of-Migrants.

[44] Interpol, "Shaping a Global Response to Corruption," accessed November 24, 2024, https://www.interpol.int/News-and-Events/News/2019/Shaping-a-global-response-to-corruption.

[45] United Nations Office on Drugs and Crime, "Terrorism Prevention Branch," accessed December 9, 2024, https://www.unodc.org/unodc/en/terrorism/index.html.

[46] United Nations Office on Drugs and Crime, "Director-General of the United Nations Office at Vienna and Executive Director of the UN Office on Drugs and Crime Takes Office," accessed November 3, 2024, https://www.unodc.org/lpo-brazil/en/frontpage/2020/02/director-general-of-the-united-nations-office-at-vienna-and-executive-director-of-the-un-office-on-drugs-and-crime-takes-office.html.

[47] United Nations Economic and Social Council (ECOSOC), United Nations Convention Against Illicit Traffic in Narcotic Drugs and Psychotropic Substances (December 19, 1988).

forfeiture, mutual legal assistance, co-operation among the law enforcement agencies of member states, control of precursors, essential chemicals, and crop eradication.

To better address the problem of the internationalization and sophistication of criminal groups, UN member states adopted the Naples Political Declaration and the Global Action Plan against Organized Transnational Crime[48] (at the World Ministerial Conference on Organized Transnational Crime held in Naples in 1994). The Naples Action Plan lays emphasis on the member states' national combating capacities as well as on international co-operation against transnational organized crime and its effective prevention.

Moreover, the UN CICP was requested (by the resolution of the UN GA 53/111, December 1998[49]) to further its tasks by preparing and conducting an open-end Intergovernmental Ad-Hoc Committee(s) on Elaboration of a comprehensive International Convention against Transnational Organized Crime and three additional instruments, to which Poland made a first draft in 1998. Between January 1999 and the end of October 2000, as many as 11 Ad Hoc meetings (minimum two-week duration each) were held in Vienna, with an average participation of 140 delegations of states and organizations.

Thus, a final text of the Convention was verified on the closing day of the 10th Session of the Ad Hoc Committee (its 177th meeting), on 28th of July 2000.

Additional instruments include: (i) Protocol to prevent, suppress and punish Trafficking in persons, especially Women and Children supplementing the UNTOC (ii) Protocol against the Smuggling of Migrants by Land, Air and Sea[50], supplementing the same Convention; and finally (iii) Protocol against the Illicit Manufacturing of and Trafficking in Firearms, their Parts and Components, and Ammunition supplementing the same Convention[51].

---

[48] United Nations, Vienna Declaration on Crime and Justice: Meeting the Challenges of the Twenty-First Century, 10th United Nations Congress on the Prevention of Crime and the Treatment of Offenders, Vienna, April 2000.

[49] United Nations General Assembly, Resolution A/RES/53/111 (January 20, 1999).

[50] United Nations, Protocol Against the Smuggling of Migrants by Land, Sea and Air, Supplementing the United Nations Convention Against Transnational Organized Crime (New York, November 15, 2000), entered into force January 28, 2004.

[51] United Nations General Assembly, Protocol Against the Illicit Manufacturing of and Trafficking in Firearms, Their Parts and Components, and Ammunition, Supplementing the United Nations Convention Against Transnational Organized Crime, A/RES/55/255 (May 31, 2001).

The High-level Political Signing conference was scheduled for December 11-15, 2000[52] (UN GA Res. 54/129), following September's Millennium Assembly Convention approval.

So far, over 193 countries have signed the Convention[53], 185 the Protocol to Prevent, Suppress and Punish Trafficking in Persons[54], and 154 the Protocol against Smuggling of migrants[55]. The Convention and the two protocols entered into force between late 2003 and early 2004. The only exception was the "Firearms" protocol, entering into force as late as mid 2005 (with currently 126 parties[56]).

To ensure compliance with the Convention and its protocols, up to 10 sessions have been held by UNTOC member states since 2020[57]. In 2018, a review mechanism was established for the implementation of the Convention[58]. Of particular interest was the session held in 2020, which adopted the self-assessment questionnaires for a review of the implementation of the Convention and the Protocols and the guidelines for conducting the country reviews. A series of resolutions was also adopted aimed at promoting international cooperation against arms trafficking, or implementation measures in the fight against trafficking in human beings. In this regard, it encourages the private sector to establish proper due diligence to end human trafficking in production chains. Finally, it also recommends that efforts be focused on other highly topical crimes, such as the misappropriation of

---

[52] United Nations General Assembly, High-level Political Signing Conference for the United Nations Convention Against Transnational Organized Crime, A/RES/54/129 (January 28, 2000).

[53] United Nations Office on Drugs and Crime (UNODC), "Information on the United Nations Convention Against Transnational Organized Crime (UNTOC)," accessed July 17, 2025, https://www.unodc.org/unodc/en/organized-crime/intro/UNTOC.html.

[54] United Nations, "United Nations Treaty Collection," accessed July 17, 2025, https://treaties.un.org/Pages/ViewDetails.aspx?src=TREATY&mtdsg_no=XVIII-12-a&chapter=18

[55] United Nations, "United Nations Treaty Collection", accessed July 17, 2025, https://treaties.un.org/pages/viewdetails.aspx?src=ind&mtdsg_no=xviii-12-a&chapter=18

[56] United Nations, "United Nations Treaty Collection", accessed July 17, 2025, https://treaties.un.org/pages/ViewDetails.aspx?src=TREATY&mtdsg_no=XVIII-12-b&chapter=18&clang=_en

[57] United Nations Office on Drugs and Crime (UNODC), "Conference of the Parties to the United Nations Convention Against Transnational Organized Crime," accessed March 23, 2021, https://www.unodc.org/unodc/en/treaties/CTOC/resolutions-and-decisions-conference-of-the-parties-to-the-united-nations-convention-against-transnational-organized-crime.html#COP5.

[58] Global Initiative Against Transnational Organized Crime, "UNTOC Review Mechanism," accessed November 24, 2024, https://globalinitiative.net/analysis/untoc-review-mechanism-one-year-to-go/.

medical products, or those that affect the environment and are carried out by international criminal organizations.

A multidimensional international strategy - centered on asset recovery, corporate accountability, and judicial cooperation - is essential to address these emerging threats, as it will be analyzed in the next chapter.

Chapter 2

The Main Anti-Crime Measures Provided for in the Palermo Convention

The Palermo Convention became essential in the global effort to tackle the problem of organized crime and established the mechanisms and rules that helped countries improve their ability to prosecute and fight international criminal organizations[1]. The activities of criminal networks that operate across borders can disrupt societies, economies, and the rule of law worldwide. With the adoption of the Palermo Convention, nearly all states in the world agreed on a legally binding framework designed to improve cooperation and strengthen their capacity[2] in the global fight against criminal networks that operate beyond national jurisdictions. It establishes a binding legal framework for transnational crimes, replacing earlier soft-law measures aimed mainly at providing guidance on domestic crime prevention and criminal justice measures[3].

The Palermo Convention recognizes that criminal enterprises often exploit legal and corporate structures to facilitate their activities and places particular emphasis on the responsibility and potential liability of businesses and corporations. Moreover, the Palermo Convention is further enhanced by three crucial protocols: The Trafficking Protocol, which focuses on the fight against human trafficking; the Migrant Smuggling Protocol, aimed at preventing and combating the smuggling of migrants; and the Firearms Protocol, which addresses the illicit manufacturing and trafficking of firearms, their components, and ammunition, aimed at curtailing organized crime, terrorism, and conflict.

These three protocols strengthened the global response to transnational crime by offering a comprehensive framework for addressing specific aspects of these criminal activities.

---

[1] Juan Pablo Soriano, "Gobernanza Global Contra la Delincuencia Transnacional: La UE y la Convención de Palermo," *Revista CIDOB d'Afers Internacionals*, no. 108 (2015): 142.

[2] Ian Tennant, "Fulfilling the Promise of Palermo? A Political History of the UN Convention Against Transnational Organized Crime," *Journal of Illicit Economies and Development* 2, no. 1 (2020): 53.

[3] Tennant, "Fulfilling the Promise of Palermo?" 61.

The Palermo Convention and its Protocols marked a key moment in the international effort to combat transnational organized crime. They introduced a comprehensive set of measures to strengthen nations' capabilities to identify, pursue, and dismantle criminal organizations. It recognized the international dimensions of organized crime and emphasized the importance of cross-border cooperation.

The UNTOC serves as a mandatory legislative and conceptual model for signatory states, aimed at enhancing global prevention and combating organized crime across the major dimensions: punishment, protection, and prevention[4]. The Palermo Convention emerged as a proactive response to the growing sophistication of criminal networks exploiting the new opportunities that have arisen from globalization. What distinguishes the UNTOC is its foresight - recognizing the need for global measures in order to be able to fight against transnational crime.

The ground-breaking Convention represented the first comprehensive effort to address transnational organized crime. In addition to defining organized crime, states parties committed themselves to criminalize certain offenses that were not pursued uniformly in every country, such as the laundering of proceeds of crime and the participation in a criminal group. Moreover, the Palermo Convention obligates states parties to implement several measures to combat organized crime. It highlights the importance of the protection of victims or witnesses of transnational crimes, anti-money laundering initiatives and the confiscation of the proceeds of crime. It also encourages states to enact national laws in order to criminalize some crimes that were not internationally recognized, and promotes international cooperation in criminal matters, emphasizing the crucial role of prevention and public awareness. Finally, it recognizes the potential liability of corporations in the fight against crimes such as money laundering or trafficking in human beings.

2.1. International Cooperation as an Instrument in the Fight Against Transnational Organized Crime

International legal cooperation has developed over centuries, building on long-standing traditions of inter-state collaboration. An early example of extradition

---

[4] Artur Airapetean and Andreaa Corsei, "International Legal Framework on Human Trafficking," *Acta Universitatis Danubius* 18, no. 3 (2022): 3.

treaties is the ancient Treaty between Egyptian Pharaoh Ramses II and Hittite King Hattusili[5] - a landmark extradition agreement whose provisions are still reflected in the archives of the British Museum and the Karnak Temple in Luxor, Egypt.

Historically, the theatre of judicial collaboration predominantly featured interactions between sovereign entities. In earlier epochs, the focal point was cooperation between governments. Although the first signs of transnational crime can be traced back to the industrial revolution[6], it was not until the latter part of the 20th century that scholars began acknowledging the imperative of individual rights in extradition proceedings.

Traditionally, states approached international cooperation in criminal matters with caution, driven either by mistrust or a determination to safeguard their *ius puniendi* - the sovereign right to punish. Collaboration was confined to cases of extradition and the processing of letters rogatory[7]. However, in the contemporary era, such limited cooperation is no longer sufficient against the complexities of modern-day crime. Therefore, international collaboration has undergone a transformative evolution - from the early enforcement of foreign sentences to a myriad of possibilities for cooperation, often involving direct intervention by judicial bodies.

A crucial moment in this evolution was the contemplation of procedures enabling the movement of judicial authorities from the requesting states to the requested states. This shift allowed for direct involvement in procedural investigative measures - a crucial development in tackling transnational crime effectively.

Classical judicial cooperation operated on reciprocity and double criminality[8], often by diplomatic channels through Ministries of Foreign Affairs. The traditional approach resulted in international judicial cooperation that was slow and limited, with diplomats taking on roles that should be reserved for judges. In Europe, the trajectory of cooperation evolved from the abandonment of reciprocity to the formation of bilateral and multilateral treaties. In 1959, the Council of Europe's Convention on Mutual Assistance

[5] S. Langdon and Alan H. Gardiner, "The Treaty of Alliance Between Ḫattušili, King of the Hittites, and the Pharaoh Ramesses II of Egypt," *The Journal of Egyptian Archaeology* 6, no. 3 (July 1920): 179–205.

[6] Ivett Csontos-Nagy, "International Criminal Cooperation in the Shadow of the Coronavirus Pandemic," *AARMS* 22, no. 1 (2023): 35.

[7] Csontos-Nagy, "International Criminal Cooperation," 35.

[8] Stefano Betti, "New Prospects for Interstate Cooperation in Criminal Matters: The Palermo Convention," *International Criminal Law Review* (2003): 172.

in Criminal Matters was signed,[9] a significant step towards achieving greater international cooperation in criminal matters among Council of Europe member states, and open to third parties[10]. By fostering collaboration in criminal matters, it aimed to overcome legal barriers and enhance international cooperation. It introduced common rules for mutual legal assistance, pioneering a standardized approach that facilitated smoother collaboration in criminal investigations and prosecutions. Moreover, it provided an extensive and comprehensive framework covering a wide array of legal assistance measures. This comprehensive scope addressed various aspects, such as the execution of letters rogatory, service of documents, intervention of witnesses, and exchange of information, streamlining the process for member states.

At the global level, the 1988 UN Convention against illicit drug trafficking[11] marked a renaissance in classical judicial cooperation, but it was not until the UNTOC that the UN directly addressed transnational organized crime, emphasizing the imperative of coordinated global efforts[12].

The Palermo Convention introduced innovative measures emphasizing a comprehensive and integrated approach to international cooperation. The various dimensions established by the Palermo Convention have two common elements. The first requires states to set up minimum legal structures, such as central authorities or national contact points; the second element calls on states to cooperate as fully as possible within their capacities. It outlines[13] cooperative strategies addressing extradition, transfer of sentenced persons, mutual legal assistance, joint investigations, special investigative techniques, and transfer of criminal proceedings.

The UNTOC facilitates extradition for offenses covered by its provisions. It places emphasis on dual criminality and the importance of fair treatment and consultation between involved states. It also encourages member states to consider agreements for the transfer of individuals serving sentences for the offenses covered under the Convention[14]. The aim is to transfer persons

---

[9] Council of Europe, European Convention on Mutual Assistance in Criminal Matters, European Treaty Series No. 30 (Strasbourg, April 20, 1959).

[10] Council of Europe, "Chart of Signatures and Ratifications of Treaty 30," accessed November 11, 2024, https://www.coe.int/en/web/conventions/full-list?module=signatures-by-treaty&treatynum=030.

[11] United Nations, United Nations Convention Against Illicit Traffic in Narcotic Drugs and Psychotropic Substances (December 19, 1988).

[12] Betti, "New Prospects," 164-165.

[13] United Nations, United Nations Convention Against Transnational Organized Crime (*UNTOC)*, Articles 16–21.

[14] The Convention offenses are, according to Article 10, the criminalization of participation in organized criminal groups (5), money laundering (6), corruption (8), and obstruction of

sentenced in a foreign country to their home country, fostering collaboration in the rehabilitation and punishment of offenders. The transfer of sentenced persons is foreseen as an important means of cooperation to prevent and combat crime, as recognized by the United Nations Convention against Illicit Traffic in Narcotic Drugs and Psychotropic Substances of 1988, the Palermo Convention, and the Convention against Corruption. Allowing for the transfer of sentenced persons may be particularly useful in achieving the proper and effective administration of justice especially when extradition is refused on the sole basis of nationality.

The Palermo Convention mandates member states to provide extensive legal assistance to each other in investigations, prosecutions, and judicial proceedings related to convention offenses[15]. The provisions cover various forms of assistance, including evidence collection, service of documents, and asset freezing, with an emphasis on flexibility and confidentiality. Special mention should be made of each state party's creation of central authorities. Each State Party is obliged to designate a central authority responsible for receiving requests for assistance and executing or transmitting them to the competent authority. This has numerous benefits, such as avoiding duplication of efforts and creating a network of cooperation experts. But it also enables Interpol to be called upon in cases of urgent need and to be used as a conduit for communications for international legal assistance.

States are urged to establish joint investigative bodies through agreements or conduct ad-hoc joint investigations, respecting the sovereignty of the host state[16]. This collaborative approach is essential for addressing issues related to investigations, prosecutions, or judicial proceedings across multiple jurisdictions.

States are also encouraged to adopt measures allowing controlled delivery and other special investigative techniques to combat organized crime effectively[17]. Agreements between states are encouraged, ensuring adherence to principles of sovereign equality and jurisdiction.

---

justice (23). Additionally, the Convention defines "serious crime" (2) as any conduct that carries a minimum penalty of four years of imprisonment, thereby reinforcing the framework for international cooperation in addressing these significant issues.

[15] United Nations, United Nations Convention against Transnational Organized Crime *(UNTOC)*, art. 18.

[16] United Nations Convention Against Transnational Organized Crime (UNTOC), art. 19.

[17] United Nations Convention Against Transnational Organized Crime (UNTOC), art. 20.

Member states of the Palermo Convention are prompted to consider transferring proceedings for convention offenses when it serves the interests of justice, particularly in cases involving multiple jurisdictions[18].

But the Palermo Convention does not cover all the international cooperation tools and it operates in tandem with several other international agreements. There exists a global framework for combating organized crime. Examples of these international treaties are the Inter-American Convention on Mutual Legal Assistance[19], the American Model Regulations on Money Laundering, the European Convention on Laundering[20], the Financial Action Task Force Recommendations[21], and various regional and bilateral agreements.

International cooperation is a key element in effectively fighting transnational crimes. Building trust among countries is essential to ensuring effective collaboration. This trust comes from shared goals, mutual respect, a commitment to fundamental rights, and confidence in each other's legal systems.

Within the EU, the main legislation on international criminal cooperation was the Convention on Mutual Legal Assistance in Criminal Matters[22], replaced by the EIO[23]. This transformation underscores a solid foundation for international cooperation within the European Union, marking a departure from traditional hesitancy toward collaboration in criminal matters. Such evolution is imperative to effectively address emerging manifestations of organized crime that traverse national borders, with a pivotal shift from the principle of cooperation by request to a compelling obligation of recognition and enforcement.

---

[18] United Nations Convention Against Transnational Organized Crime (UNTOC), art. 21.

[19] Organization of American States (OAS), Inter-American Convention on *Extradition* (February 25, 1981).

[20] Council of Europe, Council of Europe Convention on Laundering, Search, Seizure and Confiscation of the Proceeds from Crime and on the Financing of Terrorism, CETS No. 198 (Warsaw, May 16, 2005).

[21] Financial Action Task Force (FATF), "The FATF Recommendations," accessed November 24, 2024, https://www.fatf-gafi.org/en/publications/Fatfrecommendations/Fatf-recommendations.html.

[22] Council of Europe, Convention Established by the Council in Accordance with Article 34 of the Treaty on European Union, on Mutual Assistance in Criminal Matters Between the Member States of the European Union, Official Journal of the European Union L 197 (July 12, 2000).

[23] European Union, Directive 2014/41/EU of the European Parliament and of the Council of April 3, 2014, Regarding the European Investigation Order in Criminal Matters, Official Journal of the European Union L 130 (May 1, 2014): 1–36.

2.2. Protection of Victims of Transnational Crimes

Before the Palermo Convention, the 1985 Declaration of Basic Principles of Justice for Victims of Crime and Abuse of Power[24] was the most significant international instrument regarding the protection of victims of transnational crimes. This Declaration represented a crucial milestone in the protection of victims within the framework of criminal justice. It established fundamental principles to safeguard the rights of victims.

The Declaration defined victims without regard to the identity of the perpetrator or familial ties. It emphasized fair treatment, promoting compassion, dignity, and prompt redress[25]. The document advocated for accessible legal mechanisms, ensuring victims were informed of their rights throughout the judicial process.

Restitution was a key focus[26], calling for fair restitution from offenders, including the return of property and compensation, even addressing environmental harm. The principles highlighted compensation, urging states to provide financial aid, especially in significant harm or death cases.

The importance of comprehensive assistance was emphasized, including material, medical, and psychological support for victims[27]. The principles also extended to victims of abuse of power, defining them as those harmed by acts violating human rights norms. The Declaration encouraged legal remedies, including incorporating norms into national law. Periodic legislative reviews were recommended as well as the development of appropriate rights and remedies for victims of abuses of power. The Declaration prioritized victim rights, fair treatment, restitution, compensation, and comprehensive assistance.

These principles represented a significant shift, acknowledging victims as passive recipients of justice and active participants deserving respect, support, and redress. Central to these principles was the recognition of victims' right to access justice, to receive fair treatment, and to be informed and supported throughout legal proceedings. Furthermore, it underscored the need for reparations and assistance.

As globalization evolved, the Palermo Convention became essential to address the challenges posed by the new kind of transnational crimes. In this

---

[24] United Nations, Declaration of Basic Principles of Justice for Victims of Crime and Abuse of Power, A/RES/40/34 (November 29, 1985).

[25] Declaration of Basic Principles of Justice for Victims of Crime and Abuse of Power, art. 1.

[26] Ibid., art. 8.1.

[27] Ibid., arts. 14–17.

context, the Palermo Convention signified a change in thinking in the approach to global justice by placing victims at the center of its strategies, thereby making them essential actors in the fight against transnational crime. Each State Party is obliged to take measures, within the limits of its resources, to protect witnesses, as well as their family members and associates, from potential retaliation or intimidation. The multifaceted nature of this protection ranges from physical security considerations to non-disclosure or restricted disclosure of the identity and whereabouts of witnesses, striking a delicate balance between the imperative of witness safety and the recognized rights of the accused, including the right to due process. Moreover, the Palermo Convention introduces a nuanced approach to witness testimony, establishing procedural frameworks for physical protection, possible relocation, and employing communication technologies such as video conferencing. Such provisions, while emphasizing the safety of witnesses, underline the need to uphold the legal rights of defendants.

In recognition of the global nature of transnational crimes, states are urged to explore collaborative arrangements for witness relocation, a measure that transcends national borders to pursue comprehensive witness protection.

The Palermo Convention reinforces the foundational principles set out in the Declaration of Basic Principles of Justice for Victims of Crime and Abuse of Power, providing a more complete framework for justice and protection of victims of transnational crimes[28].

The Palermo Convention sets out a robust framework for safeguarding witnesses involved in criminal proceedings related to its covered offenses[29].

The Palermo Convention also mandates that states take measures to provide comprehensive assistance and protection to victims of covered offenses[30]. This includes protection from threats or intimidation. Furthermore, it establishes procedures for victims to access compensation and restitution, ensuring their participation and representation in criminal proceedings.

Comparatively, the Declaration of Basic Principles emphasizes victim rights, fair treatment, and comprehensive assistance, but the Palermo Convention goes further by specifying measures for protection against retaliation and intimidation. It also introduces an explicit provision for victims' access to compensation and restitution. However, it should be highlighted that the Palermo Convention contains notable omissions, such as

---

[28] United Nations, Declaration of Basic Principles of Justice for Victims of Crime and Abuse of Powe. Op.cit

[29] United Nations, United Nations Convention against Transnational Organized Crime, art. 24.

[30] Ibid., art. 25.

the right to legal assistance, protection of privacy, and state compensation. The most notable omission, and one that has been the subject of well-founded criticism, is the absence of the right to be informed about the proceedings[31]. The Palermo Convention strongly emphasizes international cooperation, encouraging states to enter into agreements for the relocation of protected persons. This underscores the global dimension of combating transnational organized crime and the need for collaborative efforts in ensuring the safety of witnesses and victims.

While the Declaration of Basic Principles provides a foundational framework for victim protection, the Palermo Convention advances these principles by introducing specific and detailed measures for witness and victim protection in the context of transnational organized crime.

Beyond the Palermo Convention, the protection of human rights is further fortified by additional international treaties. These treaties contribute to the comprehensive coverage and safeguarding of victims' well-being, extending rights that go beyond the scope of the Palermo Convention. Examples of these treaties are the International Covenant on Civil and Political Rights[32], the Convention on the Elimination of All Forms of Discrimination against Women[33] (CEDAW), and the Convention on the Rights of the Child[34] (CRC). Each of these instruments adds an additional layer of protection, emphasizing various facets of human rights that are integral to the overall well-being of victims of organized crime.

In the collective framework of international law, these treaties complement and reinforce the principles enshrined in the Palermo Convention. Together, they form a comprehensive network of safeguards for victims globally, addressing diverse aspects of human rights violations and providing a robust foundation for the protection and well-being of those affected by organized crime.

---

[31] Jan J. M. van Dijk, "Empowering Victims of Organized Crime: On the Concurrence of the Palermo Convention with the UN Declaration on Basic Principles of Justice for Victims," *International Review of Victimology* 9 (2002): 23.

[32] United Nations General Assembly, International Covenant on Civil and Political Rights, United Nations Treaty Series 999 (December 16, 1966): 171.

[33] United Nations General Assembly, Convention on the Elimination of All Forms of Discrimination Against Women, United Nations Treaty Series 1249 (December 18, 1979).

[34] United Nations General Assembly, Convention on the Rights of the Child, United Nations Treaty Series 1577 (November 20, 1989): 3.

2.3. Liability of Corporations

In recent years, the importance of the involvement of corporate entities in the fight against transnational crime has become an undeniable reality. As multinational corporations stretch across borders, so do the crimes that defy traditional jurisdictions; human trafficking, bribery, environmental exploitation, and more. This introduces a critical imperative: the pursuit of criminal liability for enterprises engaged in transnational offenses. How can the international community ensure accountability for corporations that operate across borders?

Fueled by the capital movements worldwide and the borderless nature of commerce, transnational crimes pose a formidable challenge to conventional legal structures. Considering this context, the need to hold corporations accountable surfaces as a key component in the collective effort to address offenses that transcend geographical boundaries. Such accountability is vital to ensure that corporations play their part in combating transnational crime effectively.

National legal systems often face challenges when dealing with crimes that cross borders, such as human trafficking, where a transnational element is usually present. To effectively address these issues, it is crucial to hold businesses accountable for their role in transnational crime.

Companies should not be regarded as passive participants in the fight against these crimes; they can and should be held responsible for their involvement in such crimes.

Businesses must recognize their responsibility in this context. Given their significant influence, they cannot overlook the possibility of inadvertently being involved in or facilitating transnational crimes. Companies must adopt ethical practices to prevent being used as instruments for criminal activities. However, merely having ethical guidelines is insufficient. Enterprises must work diligently to avoid any association between their business practices and criminal acts. They cannot be passive observers regarding their supply chains or subsidiaries; they must take full responsibility for their global impact. Traditional legal structures, developed before globalization, struggle to address crimes that are committed globally. Whether criminal, civil, or administrative liability on enterprises, imposing liability on enterprises is a crucial mechanism to bridge this gap, ensuring that these entities are held accountable for their actions, and demanding corporate responsibility becomes crucial in the fight against crimes that undermine global justice. However, different legal traditions, economic interests, and ongoing debates about the scope of corporate responsibility make this a complex challenge. The path toward recognizing corporate criminal liability has been introduced slowly. Its origins can be traced back to early legal and religious doctrines, gradually evolving over centuries into today's growing consensus that companies can - and should - be held responsible when they play a role in serious crimes.

The idea that societies could not be held accountable for the actions of their members dates to the 13th century. It was Pope Innocent IV who laid the foundation by articulating the principle that a legal entity cannot be held blameworthy (*societas delinquere non potest*, a legal entity cannot be blameworthy). This doctrine was formulated to prevent the excommunication of societies from being held liable for the actions of individual members [35]. Originating from ecclesiastical authority, this principle slowly entered European legal systems. For centuries, the traditional view held that guilt was solely an individual matter. This began to change in the 19th century when the Common Law system, rooted in England, challenged the old paradigm and led the way in establishing corporate criminal liability[36].

In 1950, the Netherlands held companies accountable under criminal law for the first time. This shift set off a chain reaction that transformed legal systems in many Civil Law countries[37]. Transnational crimes manifest in many forms, and corporations are involved in various ways. Genocide, crimes against humanity, human trafficking, corruption, and environmental crimes are just a few examples. By identifying branches at higher risk of being used in committing crimes, we can better grasp the challenges we face.

In an international setting with no uniform approach to corporate liability, the Palermo Convention took a significant step by requiring that corporations be held liable for the crimes covered by the Convention. This was a historic step because, until then, holding companies accountable was not widely accepted. Article 10 of the Palermo Convention clarifies that corporations can be involved in these crimes and urges countries to establish laws that impose liability on companies. This change means that civil, criminal, or administrative accountability extends to individual wrongdoers and the companies that enable or profit from these crimes.

---

[35] Dominik Brodowski, Manuel Espinoza de los Monteros de la Parra, and Klaus Tiedemann, *Regulating Corporate Criminal Liability: An Introduction* (Cham: Springer International Publishing, 2014), 1.

[36] Kathleen F. Brickey, "Corporate Criminal Accountability: A Brief History and Observation," *Washington University Law Quarterly* 60 (1982): 393–397.

[37] Organisation for Economic Co-operation and Development (OECD), *Liability of Legal Persons for Corruption in Eastern Europe and Central Asia* (Paris: OECD Publishing, 2015), 9.

The impact of corporations and multinationals on today's global landscape is undeniable. These companies generate significant benefits for states. They also need to operate ethically and with a human rights commitment. Crime prevention must be a core part of their business practices, requiring constant monitoring and control of their actions.

States need to hold these entities accountable for what happens within their ranks. Companies should adopt clear compliance measures to help them prevent criminal behavior within their operations. If they fail to do so, they risk not only legal penalties but also severe damage to their reputation. For example, a company involved in crimes like human trafficking or terrorism may suffer catastrophic reputational harm, even if legal consequences follow.

Recognizing the need to combat transnational crimes, the Palermo Convention emphasizes that states must implement measures to hold corporations accountable. This international agreement highlights the importance of legal frameworks that can prevent, investigate, and punish cross-border crimes. In establishing corporate liability for transnational crimes, the Convention aims to build a robust system that punishes misconduct and serves as a deterrent.

Beyond the Palermo Convention, there are other international instruments that to some extent establish the framework of corporate liability, reflecting the global commitment to fostering responsible business practices and ensuring accountability for corporate misconduct. Among these instrumental threads, the United Nations Guiding Principles on Business and Human Rights[38] stand prominently, delineating expectations for corporations to uphold and respect human rights across all facets of their operations.

The United Nations Guiding Principles, often referred to as the "Ruggie Principles[39]," represent a landmark document in the sphere of corporate responsibility. Developed by Professor John Ruggie, the Guiding Principles outline the three-pillar framework of the State's duty to protect human rights, the corporate responsibility to respect human rights, and the need for effective remedies for those affected by human rights abuses. These principles serve as a global compass, guiding corporations towards ethical conduct and emphasizing the intrinsic connection between business activities and human rights considerations.

---

[38] United Nations Office of the High Commissioner for Human Rights, *Guiding Principles on Business and Human Rights: Implementing the United Nations "Protect, Respect and Remedy" Framework* (New York and Geneva: United Nations, 2011).

[39] John Sherman, *Beyond CSR: The Story of the UN Guiding Principles on Business and Human Rights* (Cambridge, MA: Harvard Kennedy School, March 2020).

Complementing these guidelines, the Organization for Economic Cooperation and Development (OECD) Guidelines for Multinational Enterprises[40] incorporate an additional dimension to the complex landscape of corporate responsibility. The OECD Guidelines articulate principles of responsible business conduct, emphasizing the pivotal role of corporations in not only avoiding harm but actively contributing to sustainable development.

The International Criminal Court (hereinafter ICC), although mainly focused on prosecuting individuals for serious international crimes, has also taken part in discussions about corporate responsibility. It supports the idea that companies should be held accountable for their involvement in major offenses. This shows a change in the way international law sees corporations, accepting that they can be involved in and responsible for actions that go against important international legal principles

A closer examination of this framework illustrates how these instruments operate in concert to define and influence corporate responsibility. The combined strength of the UN Guiding Principles, OECD Guidelines, and the evolving approach of the ICC provides a solid basis for a well-rounded strategy on corporate liability. Together, these instruments offer unique perspectives that come together to form a coherent set of standards and mechanisms aimed at ensuring that corporations operate ethically, respect human rights, and are held accountable for any deviation from these principles.

2.4. Confiscation of Proceeds of Crime

Organized crime is fundamentally driven by profit, and effectively combating it means cutting off the financial gains that fuel these activities. This concept has been recognized for a long time - before the Palermo Convention, the Financial Action Task Force (FATF) and its Forty Recommendations were already emphasizing the importance of targeting criminal profits[41].

The FATF was established in 1989 and quickly became a key player in the global fight against money laundering and terrorist financing. Comprised of member countries and regional organizations, the task force created a set of

---

[40] Organisation for Economic Co-operation and Development (OECD), "Responsible Business Conduct," accessed November 24, 2024, https://www.oecd.org/corporate/mne/.

[41] Financial Action Task Force (FATF), accessed September 13, 2024, https://www.fatf-gafi.org/.

detailed recommendations to help countries put adequate measures in place to counter illicit financial activity. The Forty Recommendations - first issued in 1990 and regularly updated - offer a framework of legal, regulatory, and operational actions to combat money laundering on a global scale. They guide countries with different legal systems and financial structures in tackling these threats in ways that work for their specific circumstances.

As the international community grappled with the complexities of transnational crime, it became clear that a more targeted approach was needed. This realization led to a dedicated focus on seizing the illicit proceeds of crime, an issue addressed directly within the Palermo Convention.

Articles 12 to 15 of the Convention lay out a comprehensive legal structure for dealing with transnational organized crime, specifically by confiscating and disposing of assets linked to criminal activities.

Article 12 requires states parties to adopt measures in their domestic legal systems that make it easier to confiscate proceeds from crimes covered by the Convention. This includes taking ownership of property, equipment, or other tools used in these offenses. The article calls for measures to identify, trace, freeze, or seize such assets, even when mixed with legally obtained property.

Article 13 introduces the concept of international cooperation for confiscation. It sets out the responsibilities for a State Party that receives a request from another country seeking the confiscation of assets within its borders. The receiving state should either forward the request to the appropriate authority or follow the confiscation order from the requesting state. This article also stresses the importance of identifying, tracing, and freezing or seizing assets for future confiscation.

Article 14 deals with disposing of confiscated assets. It directs states parties to manage the disposal process according to their own domestic laws and administrative procedures. When a request comes from another country, priority should be given to returning assets to the requesting state - especially when doing so can help compensate victims or restore property to its legitimate owners.

Article 15 focuses on bolstering international cooperation to make the confiscation process more effective. It encourages states parties to enter into bilateral or multilateral treaties or agreements that facilitate this cooperation, while ensuring that legitimate third parties' rights are respected.

Together, articles 12 to 15 create a unified approach within the Palermo Convention. They promote collaboration among states parties to identify, trace, freeze, and ultimately confiscate assets linked to transnational organized crime and responsibly dispose of those assets.

In the pursuit of effective asset confiscation aligned with the Palermo Convention, the establishment of specialized asset recovery offices emerge as fundamental instruments. These offices play a crucial role in implementing the measures outlined in those articles of the Convention. Equipped with comprehensive access to information, these entities become instrumental in the identification, tracing, and eventual confiscation of proceeds and property associated with transnational organized crime.

International cooperation is a fundamental pillar in the effective implementation of confiscation processes. Acknowledging the complexities of tracing the proceeds and assets of crime across borders, states are urged to work together through joint investigation teams. Such collaborative efforts are essential for overcoming the inherent challenges in tracking assets that often transcend national boundaries. Quick exchange of information between states becomes imperative, emphasizing the need for robust mechanisms that facilitate timely and effective sharing of pertinent data.

To further fortify the enforcement of confiscation measures, it is highly recommended that domestic legislation clearly delineates the processes governing confiscation and seizure of property. Clarity in legal frameworks not only ensures compliance with the Palermo Convention but also enhances the efficiency and transparency of national efforts to combat transnational organized crime. The UN has reaffirmed the importance of fighting the economic dimension of transnational organized crime by strengthening efforts to address the economic dimensions and manifestations of transnational organized crime through international cooperation. This is not only a general principle but also a guideline of criminal policy that should be implemented through a series of concrete measures, such as those relating to non-conviction-based confiscation[42].

However, addressing the destination of confiscated property can lead to some practical problems in the international arena. The Council of the European Union Framework Decision 2006/783[43] provides one potential solution, offering guidance on the disposition of seized assets. Pursuant to article 16, where money has been obtained through the execution of a confiscation order, if the amount is 10,000 euros or less, it is retained by the executing state. Otherwise, 50 per cent of the amount obtained is transferred to the issuing state. However, at the international level, other alternative

---

[42] Antonio Balsamo, "Twenty Years Later: The New Perspectives of the Palermo Convention," *Dibattito* 6, no. 3 (2020): 11.

[43] Council of the European Union, Framework Decision 2006/783/JHA on the Principle of Mutual Recognition to Confiscation Orders (October 6, 2006).

arrangements should be explored. Collaborative agreements between states could involve handing over confiscated property to an international organization or sharing it among participating states. Importantly, any such international collaboration should be executed without prejudicing the obligation to address corresponding civil liabilities, ensuring a fair and equitable distribution of assets.

Chapter 3

Strengthening Global Security: A Focus on UNTOC Protocols

As discussed in earlier chapters, the Palermo Convention was a significant step forward in the fight against transnational organized crime. It not only set the parameters for what constitutes transnational crime but also laid the groundwork for strong international cooperation, put victims at the center of protection efforts, and stressed the need to lessen the impact of these crimes. The Convention's influence grew even further with the addition of three protocols, which broadened its reach.

These Protocols tackle serious issues that previously had little international oversight. They address human trafficking, the smuggling of migrants, and the trafficking of arms, which had not been previously comprehensively regulated on a global level. Unlike drug trafficking or terrorism, the crimes of the three protocols were often overlooked in domestic laws, resulting in weak international cooperation.

Each of the three protocols - the one to prevent, suppress, and punish trafficking in persons (especially women and children), the one against the smuggling of migrants by land, sea, and air, and the one targeting the illicit manufacture and trafficking of firearms, their parts, and ammunition - extends the Convention's framework. They provide targeted strategies for dealing with different types of transnational crime, reflecting the constantly changing nature of criminal behavior worldwide.

The three protocols - the Protocol to Prevent, Suppress and Punish Trafficking in Persons, Especially Women and Children; the Protocol against the Smuggling of Migrants by Land, Sea and Air; and the Protocol against the Illicit Manufacturing of and Trafficking in Firearms, Their Parts and Components and Ammunition - significantly expand the reach of the Palermo Convention. Each one addresses a specific form of transnational crime, offering targeted tools and strategies to respond to these global threats. Together, they reflect how criminal activity continues to evolve and highlight the need for international cooperation to keep pace.

3.1. Trafficking in Human Beings and Migrant Smuggling As Forms of Transnational Crime. Similarities and Differences

Before examining each Protocol in detail, we must first understand the key differences between human trafficking and migrant smuggling. These two crimes are often confused, but looking at them side by side helps clarify the specific challenges each one presents. While they are undoubtedly connected in many ways, they have distinct features that must be recognized in order to fully grasp the focus and purpose of the first and second protocols to the UNTOC[1]. Trafficking in human beings is a serious violation of the fundamental rights of its victims, while migrant smuggling, in principle, involves a breach of a country's immigration or administrative laws. Nevertheless, the harsh conditions and serious risks faced by migrants at the hands of smugglers fully justify the criminalization of this conduct. Every year, thousands of people lose their lives due to false promises and the dangerous journeys organized by smuggling networks.

Organized crime groups are vertically (hierarchically) and horizontally structured in such a manner that different sub-groups (chambers) are specialized in specific activities. The level of diversification of tasks inside the criminal organization is sufficiently high. Such task diversification aims to meet both demands: higher specialization and sophistication as well as better protection from police raids or sting operations.

In the business of trafficking in persons (long-lasting horizontal inter-dependency is very high), organized crime groups profit from both (i) the escort services themselves, and (ii) from the subsequent exploitation of the trafficked persons as workforce, who, upon transfer, are recruited for criminal purposes. This double use makes the business of trafficking in persons competitive with drug smuggling and other fast and highly lucrative criminal activities. This explains why even the biggest and most structured organized crime groups (especially transnational) have incorporated trafficking in persons into their core activities. Transnational expansion requires the permanent networking of the organization. To set up a new network, or to improve the existing one, additional recruitment must be carried out repeatedly. Therefore, in most cases, it is not the trafficked person but the

---

[1] Office to Monitor and Combat Trafficking in Persons, *Human Trafficking and Migrant Smuggling: Understanding the Difference* (Washington, DC: U.S. Department of State, June 2017). Accessed December 5, 2024. https://www.state.gov/wp-content/uploads/2019/02/272325.pdf.

organized crime group that makes the final decisions about: (i) how many people to traffic, (ii) which ethnicity, gender, skills or profile to traffic, and finally (iii) to which destination(s) – one or several countries.

Organized crime groups essentially function like any legal economic entity[2]. Consequently, the goal of organized crime is similar to that of an ordinary commercial enterprise: to gain profit. As any profit depends on the market, criminal groups enhance their productivity, efficiency, sophistication, and organization, cutting costs and risks, widening their territory, and trying to set up an exclusive monopoly in certain fields and/or on certain territory to maintain and optimize their profits. The process of profit-making and cost-cutting can put the lives of trafficked or smuggled persons at higher risk. In the face of growing demand, internal competition among organized criminal groups is rising and leading to increased violence which is exercised on both levels: internally (towards its own members) and externally (towards other gangs as well as towards the wider society).

Wishing to cover their illegal activities in trafficking and smuggling, as well as to launder generated assets afterwards, the organized crime groups often expand their activities into legitimate businesses[3] (such as newspapers/print houses, travel agencies, language summer or seasonal schools, vocational institutes, shipping companies; non-governmental humanitarian and other illicit or converted charities, and other sorts of non-profit organizations). Therefore, it becomes very hard to distinguish overt from covert activities of those groups. By doing so, the organized crime groups are fulfilling several ultimate goals: (i) better protection from eventual raids and coverage for their illegal activity (risk spreading/burden-sharing); (ii) money laundering; (iii) gradual legalization and respectability; (iv) more prominent and powerful positioning within the given society. Lastly, the role of corporations in the fight against human trafficking deserves emphasis. It is essential that companies of all sizes actively engage in combating human trafficking. Traffickers frequently rely on corporations for illicit purposes, such as the money laundering of the proceeds of crime, making it crucial to prevent the utilization of companies for human trafficking. With companies' involvement, traffickers' activities can be significantly impeded.

---

[2] United Nations Office on Drugs and Crime (UNODC), *Module 7: Models of Organized Criminal Groups*, accessed December 11, 2023, https://www.unodc.org/e4j/en/organized-crime/module-7/key-issues/groups-vs-activities.html.

[3] Kelly, R. J. "Introduction: Organized Crime Penetrations of Legitimate Businesses," in *The Upperworld and the Underworld: Criminal Justice and Public Safety*, ed. R. J. Kelly (Boston, MA: Springer, 1999).

Corporations are fundamental in addressing globalized crimes, and it should be underscored that they can and should play a vital role in preventing human trafficking.

We must also bear in mind that the lasting achievement of any parallel structure (parallel society) which organized crime tends to become (when phases of accumulation, stabilization, expansion, and monopolization are successfully met), is to legalize itself. To achieve this, the organized crime group employs all means at its disposal (ranging from hard means such as: blackmail, extortion, assassination, kidnapping, denunciation, intimidation, and racketeering; to soft means, like: corruption, humanitarian contributions, sponsorship, and voluntary donations for political and other societal campaigns, among others).

Facing increasing competition, the organized crime groups are forced to undergo certain specialization, or diversification as well as company-like fusions or synergies. Specialization, diversification, and fusions are creating a higher vertical line (along with a wider horizontal line). Apart from enlarging their market and profit shares it allows the organization for (i) better damage control capability, and (ii) minimize risk of law enforcement.

Their operational adaptability, managerial flexibility, and organizational agility make these groups hard to dismantle.

Crime groups range from individual actors to extensive networks composed of family members (or of persons from the same region, of shared language or religion), up to strictly organized, hierarchically structured and trans-continentally tied organized crime rings. Most of the operating groups are of the same ethnic origin either in their core staff or entirely. Functionally, these groups are horizontally structured from several sub-units that are specialized in a particular part or sequence of the smuggling/trafficking operation. In many cases, victims are recruited and trafficked by their own compatriots and even by their relatives. On many occasions, it may also be the victims themselves who recruit the new victims[4]. The organization is composed of diversified units, each performing specific roles independently. Each unit or element consists of one or more persons who are highly specialized, independent and with little knowledge about other parts of their own organization (in most cases, vertically they know only their direct supervisor whereas their horizontal knowledge is practically non-existent).

[4] HTCourts.org, "9 Ways Human Traffickers Recruit Their Victims," accessed December 16, 2024, https://htcourts.org/ways-human-traffickers-recruit-victims/.

Because the term "human trafficking" is often confused with "migrant smuggling," it is essential to distinguish between the two. Smuggling involves illegally helping someone cross borders, violating national immigration laws, and often putting migrants at serious risk. While trafficking and smuggling are different crimes, they sometimes overlap in practice. A deeper understanding of both phenomena is crucial to unpack their complexities and identify where they diverge and where they may intersect[5].

The relationship between smugglers and migrants usually ends once they reach their destination. It is essentially a business transaction - one in which the smuggler profits from the migrant's vulnerable situation. In contrast, in cases of trafficking in human beings, the abuse and exploitation typically begin after the victim arrives at their destination. This begins a prolonged period of coercion, control, and exploitation.

The term 'trafficking' in English refers specifically to trade, particularly illicit trade[6]. Key aspects of trafficking in persons[7] include:

(i) The involvement of an intermediary, a trafficker, who facilitates the process by providing transport.
(ii) Traffickers receive compensation under long-term arrangements.
(iii) Border crossings are often either illegal or seemingly legal, exploiting established legal structures in host countries, such as language summer schools or vocational institutes, concealing their true (illegal) intentions. Although trafficking can occur within the same state, victims are commonly trafficked across borders.
(iv) Upon arrival in a host country, migrants, with or without their consent, are victims of exploitation. Consent on the part of the victim is irrelevant. There can be no valid consent to be exploited.
(v) The profit in trafficking is derived not solely from a transportation fee but from long-term exploitation.
(vi) In most cases, trafficked persons seemingly make a free choice to enter or stay in a country illegally.

---

[5] Paolo Campana and Federico Varese, "Exploitation in Human Trafficking and Smuggling," *European Journal of Crime Policy and Research* 22 (2016): 89–105.

[6] United Nations Office on Drugs and Crime (UNODC), "Trafficking in Persons and Smuggling of Migrants," accessed December 11, 2023, https://www.unodc.org/e4j/en/organized-crime/module-3/key-issues/trafficking-in-persons.html.

[7] UNODC, "Trafficking in Persons."

The English legal term "smuggling" refers to illicit or illegal import or export. Smuggling of persons, accordingly, involves the illegal transportation of human beings from the source country to the destination or host country. Characteristics of the smuggling of persons include:

(i) An intermediary, a smuggler, who facilitates border crossing.
(ii) Crossing of the border is either illegal or seemingly legal.
(iii) Smuggling does not entail a component of extended exploitation, and the escort fee is paid under short-term arrangements.

Four distinguishing elements that set trafficking of human beings apart from migrant smuggling are:

(i) Long-term exploitation and usage of the trafficked person.
(ii) Inter-dependency forming a strong linkage between trafficked victims and organized crime groupings.
(iii) Eligibility for further networking.
(iv) Often, trafficking itself is not a voluntary movement, whereas smuggled persons typically move voluntarily.

Trafficking in human beings and migrant smuggling remain a serious worldwide threat. Criminal organizations continue to see both phenomena as significant business opportunities incorporating the 'trafficking in' and 'smuggling of' persons in their agendas, as it turns out to be:

(i) low investment (ii) high profit[8] gained (iii) lenient punishment (e.g., compared to drug trafficking, the penalties for trafficking in and smuggling of persons are still considerably lower or even non-existent in many countries).

A typical criminal organization involved in the business of 'Trafficking in' and 'smuggling of persons' is comprised of the following elements or units (cells)[9]:

---

[8] United Nations Office on Drugs and Crime (UNODC), Transnational Crime: Let's Put Them Out of Business, accessed December 11, 2023, https://www.unodc.org/toc/en/crimes/human-trafficking.html.

[9] United Nations Office on Drugs and Crime (UNODC), "Human Trafficking: Organized Crime and the Multibillion Dollar Sale of People," accessed November 29, 2024, https://www.unodc.org/unodc/en/frontpage/2012/July/human-trafficking_-organized-crime-and-the-multibillion-dollar-sale-of-people.html.

A. Recruitment unit (common for both traffickers and smugglers).

Advertises the organization and recruits new clients by using informal exchange of information (locals, friends, relatives, compatriots), up to announcements in the press or on the internet, including various kinds of overt agencies (travel agencies, summer schools, etc.); in recent years, the processes of recruitment and deception through the internet and new technologies have intensified, in cases of human trafficking such as the lover boy cases.

B. Escort unit (common for both traffickers and smugglers).

Deals with transport by land, air or waterways and takes care of every stage of the transportation phase (from the sending country, throughout transiting country/ies and to the destination – a host country). Very often this unit has sub-units which further specialize in particular sub-tasks; territory or means of transportation;

C. Corrupted officials (common for both traffickers and smugglers).

These officials, although not necessarily interconnected or known to each other, are basically acting as an integral (corrupted) unit together with members of the organized crime ring that are corrupting them. Co-operation of local officials may play a critically important role in setting up, maintaining and further permanent networking of the trafficking/smuggling structure. Hence, bribed officials in the sending, transiting or host-country are essential for the safe transfer of illegal migrants. As in other fields of organized criminal activity, corruption is an elementary part of the trafficking/smuggling business.

D. Guiding/navigation unit (common for both traffickers and smugglers).

Mostly comprised of local agents and informants who know very little about the organization and each other. This in turn minimizes the risk of law enforcement gaining access on the organization and its activities. Greater compartmentalization enables better damage control.

E. Supporting/Logistics unit (common for both traffickers and smugglers).

The task of this unit is to provide all the supporting services (safe shelter, accommodation, food, etc.). This is to prevent the illegal migrants from having any contact to the ordinary society (keeping them totally at the mercy of their traffickers). By doing so, both aims will be fulfilled: (i) protection of the operation from any police interception and eventual information leakage; as well as (ii) creating interdependency at an early stage between those trafficked and the traffickers thus enabling further long-term exploitation;

F. Debt collecting unit (common for both traffickers and smugglers).

This unit is responsible for keeping illegal migrants in the safe houses and collecting the transportation fees. Unlike the smuggling of persons– business in which this unit collects a one-off escort service fee from smuggled persons, in the business of trafficking in persons the unit is permanently collecting revenue from all illegal (or overt) businesses that the trafficked persons are recruited for. Usually, the debt rate is purposely set high which then transforms into a debt-bondage that proves to be the most effective control mechanism (further reinforcing dependency between the trafficked and the traffickers).

G. Exploiting unit(s) (traffickers only).

The number of units or sub-units depends on the number of activities that any organization is involved in (such as: exploitation of prostitution, drugs and organ smuggling, shop-window restaurants/cafes/gambling houses for money laundering, pick-pocketing, car theft, forging, begging, etc.). This unit operates entirely within the place of exploitation of victims, usually the host country/ies;

H. Re-escort unit (traffickers only).

As mentioned before, most of the victims of trafficking are re-escorted to several countries, irrespective of their will. This is especially evident in cases of exploitation of prostitution, cybercrime, terrorism-related espionage, and drug smuggling.

I. Management/Supervising unit (common for both traffickers and smugglers).

This is the single vertical unit in the explained structure, whereas all others (from A to H) are horizontal. This unit drafts, plans, finances, manages, chains, and supervises the whole operation and maintains a criminal structure that is both operable and profitable in its covert and overt segments. This unit is rarely known to the horizontal units and is hardly visible to or penetrable from the outside world (very often camouflaged by the well-established legal business, and/or protected by the prominent public figures).

There are several channels and routes for trafficking in and smuggling of persons in Europe. The routing/re-routing is permanently changing or oscillating according to several factors such as: geographical position, distance between countries of departure and destination, political and economic situation, law enforcement efforts in different areas, and an achieved degree of corruption. Organized crime groups are flexible and adaptable to any change of circumstances (sometimes changing their routes from one day to another) - e.g., when the authorities in one country improve their fight against both crimes, or intensify their legal enforcement, the groups move to another territory where they can act with greater impunity.

When expanding into new criminal areas, the new activities are often channeled through the old and already tested routes (e.g., routes used for drug trafficking are now further being used for trafficking in and smuggling of persons or human organs, or lately by the terrorist cells).

By doing so, the trafficking and smuggling organizations are directly influencing both: (i) the direction as well as (ii) the intensity and patterns of general criminal flows.

As far as trafficking in human beings is concerned, there are multiple routes, although it is impossible to know all of them or to give an accurate picture due to the very secrecy and invisibility of the crime. However, given the places of origin of the victims of trafficking in human beings detected in recent years [10], it allows us to indicate the main routes used by traffickers. A first one, which goes from sub-Saharan Africa, North Africa, and the Middle East towards Europe via southern countries such as Spain, Italy, and Greece. 2015 saw an unprecedented increase in the number of migrants across the sea and overland towards the European Union, mainly fleeing armed conflicts in the Middle East.

Subsequently, intensified controls and agreements between the EU and Turkey led many migrants and refugees to resort to smugglers to reach the EU, increasing the risk of human trafficking. The war between Russia and Ukraine has led to a significant wave of migration. Routes have also been detected from East Asia, South Asia, and the Pacific to both North America and Europe, either via Eastern Europe or via the Middle East. And finally, a route from South America to Central and North America and Europe.

---

[10] United Nations Office on Drugs and Crime (UNODC), *Global Report on Trafficking in Persons* (New York: United Nations, 2022). Accessed December 11, 2024. https://www.unodc.org/unodc/en/press/releases/2023/January/global-report-on-trafficking-in-persons-2022.html.

For their part, migrant smuggling routes are numerous and carried out in a variety of ways[11]. The most common cases are between countries in the Mekong sub-region and other parts of Central Asia on land borders. Also, in Spain, at the borders of Morocco with the Spanish cities of Ceuta and Melilla, migrants have to jump over metal fences. Another major land route is between Mexico and the US. Smugglers are also active between numerous African, Eastern European, and Central Asian borders. Particularly dangerous are borders that include jungles such as in Southeast Asia, the deserts of Africa, and the Americas. As for sea routes, the most relevant smuggling passages involving sea crossings are those across the Mediterranean Sea to southern Europe, from the Horn of Africa to the Arabian Peninsula, and across the Andaman Sea to South-East Asia. Less relevant than in the recent past are sea smuggling routes to Australia from South-East Asia.

3.2. First Protocol: Protocol to Prevent, Suppress and Punish Trafficking in Persons, Especially Women and Children

The Protocol to Prevent, Suppress, and Punish Trafficking in Persons, Especially Women and Children, supplementing the UNTOC, was adopted by the General Assembly of the United Nations on November 15, 2000[12]. It was designed to complement the UNTOC by targeting the serious crime of human trafficking, which impacts millions globally.

Human trafficking is, in fact, a way of slavery adapted to our era, albeit with new particularities as far as it is prohibited worldwide. Therefore, it is commonly referred to as modern slavery, given that criminal groups use modern means to practically enslave people, exploiting victims for personal gain. Slavery was banned during the 19th century in most of the world's countries, and international agreements were even adopted at the beginning of the 20th century. Subsequently, based on treaties aimed primarily at combating trafficking in human beings in the field of prostitution, the scope of action was widened until the 1949 Convention was enacted, which to a

---

[11] United Nations Office on Drugs and Crime (UNODC), *Global Study on Smuggling of Migrants* (New York: United Nations, 2018). Accessed September 11, 2024. https://www.unodc.org/unodc/en/data-and-analysis/glotip-2018.html.

[12] United Nations, Protocol to Prevent, Suppress and Punish Trafficking in Persons, Especially Women and Children, Supplementing the United Nations Convention against Transnational Organized Crime, November 15, 2000. Accessed November 24, 2024. https://treaties.un.org/pages/ViewDetails.aspx?src=TREATY&mtdsg_no=XVIII-12-a&chapter=18.

certain extent did address the fight against trafficking in human beings in a more decisive manner, by defining trafficking in human beings for the purpose of procuring regardless of the person's consent. The 1949 Convention marked a notable step forward by addressing human trafficking for procurement purposes, irrespective of the individual's consent. However, limited ratification by states and the Convention's narrow focus impeded its practical effectiveness. The subsequent enactment of the Palermo Protocol sought to complement the Convention, aiming to comprehensively address the global predicament of human trafficking.

Since its establishment, the Palermo Convention has had a substantial impact, prompting over 90% of nations worldwide to enact laws criminalizing human trafficking[13]. This widespread adoption underscores its status as one of the most widely embraced international treaties. Beyond its broad acceptance, the true milestone lies in its unprecedented success in formulating a universally recognized definition of human trafficking. Before the introduction of the Protocol on Trafficking in Human Beings, earlier treaties did not provide a widely accepted definition, leading to ambiguity surrounding the issue of human trafficking.

According to the Palermo Protocol[14] trafficking in persons shall mean the recruitment, transportation, transfer, harboring, or receipt of persons, by means of the threat or use of force or other forms of coercion, of abduction, of fraud, of deception, of the abuse of power or of a position of vulnerability or of the giving or receiving of payments or benefits to achieve the consent of a person having control over another person, for the purpose of exploitation. "Exploitation shall include, at a minimum, the exploitation of the prostitution of others or other forms of sexual exploitation, forced labor or services, slavery, or practices similar to slavery, servitude, or the removal of organs."

A key success of the Palermo Protocol was the establishment of a clear and widely accepted definition of human trafficking - something previous treaties had failed to achieve.

This definition catalyzed the criminalization of human trafficking in numerous countries. Preceding the Protocol, many nations refrained from penalizing trafficking, often due to a lack of awareness or understanding of the phenomenon.

---

[13] Nicole J. Siller, "Human Trafficking in International Law Before the Palermo Protocol," *Netherlands International Law Review* (2017): 2.

[14] United Nations. *United* Nations Convention Against Transnational Organized Crime (UNTOC*)*, Article 3.

The Protocol's influence extends to the enactment of legislation criminalizing human trafficking in numerous states. The definition was ground-breaking since it established a broad minimum of actions that should be considered trafficking in human beings. It expands the concept to other kinds of exploitations different to exploitation for sexual purposes. It leaves a window open for states to be able to expand the idea to other types of trafficking in human beings. It is an agreement of minimums, but it established a broad definition that should be incorporated into domestic legislation. There has been ongoing debate surrounding the criminalization of human trafficking solely within the context of transnational crime. However, the legislative guide emphasizes that states should not establish national laws that require the involvement of organized criminal groups or the crossing of borders as conditions for defining human trafficking as a criminal offense[15].

The definition of "trafficking in persons" is expansive, including various means and forms of exploitation. The inclusion of coercion, fraud, and abuse of power aims to include the diverse tactics employed by traffickers. The recruitment allows the criminalization of new techniques used by traffickers, mainly by the use of the Internet. However, there have been some critics because the definition of trafficking in human beings left the states the possibility of establishing other kinds of exploitation and it was not clearly stated what should be understood under the term "exploitation"[16]. This fact has been derived from different definitions of trafficking in human beings, which may entail some problems derived from the necessity in an international context of dual criminalization. The Palermo Protocol provides only a vague definition of exploitation, leading to uncertainty in cases such as coerced pornography[17], resulting in different domestic legislations[18]. However, the Model law defines sexual exploitation as the obtaining of financial or other benefits through the involvement of another person in…sexual services, including pornographic acts or the production of pornographic materials[19].

---

[15] Artur Airapetean and Andreaa Corsei, "International Legal Framework Regarding Human Trafficking," *Acta Universitatis Danubius* 18, no. 3 (2022): 95.

[16] Ana B. Valverde Cano, "Reexaminando la Definición de Trata de Seres Humanos del Protocolo de Palermo: La Trata como Forma de Explotación," *Estudios de Deusto* 67, no. 2 (2019): 11-12.

[17] Hope Watson, "Pornography-Based Sex Trafficking," *Vanderbilt Journal of Transnational Law* 54 (2021): 495-515.

[18] United Nations Office on Drugs and Crime (UNODC), *Model Law Against Trafficking in Persons*, August 5, 2009, 28. Accessed September 11, 2024. https://www.unhcr.org/media/model-law-against-trafficking-persons.

[19] UNODC, Model Law Against Trafficking in Persons.

There exists a robust academic discourse supporting the prosecutability of coerced pornography based on the plain language of the Protocol. It is argued that when individuals exchange money for pornographic videos depicting women who are transported and provided for sex, it constitutes the exploitation of others[20].

An exceptional feature of the protocol's legislation is its emphasis on prioritizing victims. While it may not explicitly label human trafficking as a severe infringement of human rights, it marks the first instance where international legislation places victims at the forefront. The Protocol delineates measures aimed at protecting the privacy and identity of victims, ensuring their active participation in legal proceedings, and facilitating their recovery, but in broader terms. The emphasis on tailored support, encompassing housing, counselling, and educational opportunities, reflects the complex needs of victims, with special attention to the unique circumstances of children[21]. The states parties are also urged to consider the adoption of legislative or other appropriate measures that permit victims of trafficking in persons to remain in their territory[22], but it does not establish a compulsory recovery and reflection period, which is fundamental to grant protection to victims of trafficking in human beings. For this reason, the Model Law[23] urges to adopt a recovery period that should not be less than 90 days in order to help victims and informed decision on whether to cooperate or not with the authorities. In contrast, the repatriation is explicitly foreseen and the states parties are obliged to facilitate and accept the return of a victim national or with the right of permanent residence with due regard for the safety of the victim[24].

The Palermo Protocol mandates that states develop extensive policies and programs to tackle underlying issues like poverty and underdevelopment. It advocates for collaboration with non-governmental organizations and civil society to exchange information and emphasizes the significance of training that considers human rights, as well as issues related to children and gender

---

[20]Hope Watson, "Pornography-Based Sex Trafficking: A Palermo Protocol Fit for the Internet Age," *Vanderbilt Law Review* 54 (2021): 495, 520.

[21] Protocol to Prevent, Suppress and Punish Trafficking in Persons, Especially Women and Children*, art. 6.*

[22] Protocol Against Trafficking in Persons, art. 7.

[23] United Nations Office on Drugs and Crime (UNODC), Model Law Against Trafficking in Persons, art. 30.

[24] Protocol to Prevent, Suppress and Punish Trafficking in Persons, art. 8.

sensitivity. This underscores the understanding that combating trafficking requires a multi-stakeholder approach[25].

In addressing the transnational nature of trafficking, the protocol calls for strengthen, without prejudice to international commitments, border controls and document security measures[26]. This reflects a pragmatic acknowledgment of the role of border enforcement in curbing the movement of traffickers and victims.

The Protocol also introduces a humanitarian dimension, safeguarding the rights of individuals under international law, including humanitarian and refugee conventions. The emphasis on non-discrimination is a crucial academic consideration, aligning the protocol with established principles of human rights. However, it fails to embrace a distinct human rights perspective and gender mainstreaming, essential elements found in international legislation post the Palermo Protocol. Since the promulgation of the Palermo Protocol, a comprehensive regional legal framework has emerged, integrating a criminal justice approach to trafficking with a victim-cantered and human rights-based strategy. Recognizing trafficking as both a crime and a violation of human rights implies that states bear the responsibility to respect, protect, and promote the human rights of all trafficked individuals, irrespective of their country of origin[27]. In line with this, the UN Special Rapporteur on trafficking in human beings emphasizes the importance of incorporating the human rights dimension into legislation concerning the trafficking of human beings, urging states to consider this perspective.

In addition to the UNTOC and the Palermo Protocol, it is imperative to consider various other international agreements that play a crucial role in addressing human trafficking and related offenses. Notable among these are Slavery Convention[28], the Charter of the International Military Tribunal (IMT

---

[25] Ibid., arts. 9-10.

[26] Ibid., arts. 11-13.

[27] OHCHR, UNHCR, UNICEF, UNODC, UN Women, and ILO, *Joint UN Commentary on the EU Directive: A Human Rights Based Approach* (2011), 17. Accessed September 21, 2024. https://www.unodc.org/unodc/en/human-trafficking/2012/joint-un-commentary-on-eu-directive-on-preventing-and-combating-trafficking-in-human-beings-is-launched-at-the-european-parliament.html.

[28] League of Nations, Convention to Suppress the Slave Trade and Slavery, 60 LNTS 253, Registered No. 1414 (September 25, 1926). Accessed November 24, 2024. https://www.ohchr.org/en/instruments-mechanisms/instruments/slavery-convention.

Charter, Nuremberg)[29], European Convention on Human Rights (ECHR)[30], Supplementary Convention on the Abolition of Slavery[31], International Covenant on Civil and Political Rights[32], American Convention on Human Rights[33], African Charter on Human and Peoples' Rights[34], ICC Statute[35], African Union Convention for the Protection and Assistance of Internally Displaced Persons in Africa (Kampala Convention)[36] Regarding trafficking in human beings for labor exploitation, are crucial the International Labor Organization (ILO) Conventions, specifically the ILO Forced Labor Convention[37] and its protocol, along with the ILO Abolition of Forced Labor Convention[38], both focusing on combatting forced labor and servitude. In relation to prostitution, a cornerstone in the fight against the exploitation of persons is the United Nations Convention for the Suppression of the Traffic in Persons and of the Exploitation of Others[39] (1949) and its Protocol of 1969. These instruments compel states to take punitive measures against individuals involved in the exploitation of prostitution.

Furthermore, the ICCPR explicitly prohibits activities associated with trafficking in persons, including slavery, slave trade, servitude, and forced labor.

Addressing the trafficking of women, the Convention on the Elimination of All Forms of Discrimination against Women[40] obliges states to implement appropriate measures to eradicate all forms of trafficking and the exploitation

---

[29] United Kingdom of Great Britain and Northern Ireland, United States of America, France, and Union of Soviet Socialist Republics, Charter of the International Military Tribunal (London Agreement), United Nations, August 8, 1945. Accessed November 24, 2024. https://ihl-databases.icrc.org/en/ihl-treaties/nuremberg-tribunal-charter-1945.

[30] Council of Europe, European Convention on Human Rights, art. 4(1); see also art. 15(2)

[31] United Nations, Supplementary Convention on the Abolition of Slavery, art. 1 (1956).

[32] United Nations, International Covenant on Civil and Political Rights, art. 8.

[33] Organization of American States (OAS), American Convention on Human Rights (1969), art. 6(1).

[34] African Union, African Charter on Human and Peoples' Rights, art. 5.

[35] Rome Statute of the International Criminal Court, art. 7(1)(c), 7(2)(c).

[36] African Union, African Union Convention for the Protection and Assistance of Internally Displaced Persons in Africa, October 23, 2009. Accessed November 24, 2024. https://au.int/en/treaties/african-union-convention-protection-and-assistance-internally-displaced-persons-africa.

[37] Kampala Convention, *art.* 9(1). Accessed September 29, 2024. https://au.int/sites/default/files/treaties/36846-treaty-kampala_convention.pdf.

[38] International Labour Organization (ILO*)*, Abolition of Forced Labour Convention, C105 (June 25, 1957).

[39] United Nations General Assembly, Convention for the Suppression of the Traffic in Persons and of the Exploitation of the Prostitution of Others, A/RES/317 (December 2, 1949).

[40] United Nations General Assembly, Convention for the Suppression of the Traffic in Persons and of the Exploitation of the Prostitution of Others, A/RES/317(IV) (March 21, 1950).

of women in prostitution. General Recommendation No. 19[41] recognizes trafficking as a form of violence against women, emphasizing the heightened risk of violence and abuse faced by women in such situations.

Specific provisions regarding the trafficking of children are foreseen in the Convention on the Rights of the Child[42] (1989) and the Optional Protocol on the Sale of Children, Child Prostitution, and Child Pornography[43] (2000).

On a regional level, significant strides have been made in anti-trafficking initiatives. The Council of Europe Trafficking Convention (Warsaw Convention)[44] and the Asian Trafficking Convention[45] (Kuala Lumpur) stand out as noteworthy. The COE Convention, extending beyond COE members, introduces ground-breaking elements, considering the fight against human trafficking a matter of human rights, given its violation of victims' dignity and integrity. States can be held responsible for cases of trafficking in human beings if they havn't adopted the necessary measures to prevent a case[46]. States are seen as duty-bearers, and victims as rights-holders. Moreover, the COE Convention establishes concrete protective measures for victims, including the right to compensation and a designated period for reflection. Additionally, it makes the liability of company's compulsory for cases of trafficking in persons committed by their members in instances of a lack or failure of supervision.

In contrast, the ASEAN Convention[47] incorporates several aggravating circumstances and criminalizes money laundering associated with trafficking, addresses corruption, and criminalizes the obstruction of justice. These regional agreements demonstrate a concerted effort to combat human trafficking through multifaceted and comprehensive approaches.

The Protocol has achieved considerable success, though there is still room for improvement. After the Protocol was adopted, many countries took their

---

[41] United Nations Committee on the Elimination of Discrimination Against Women (CEDAW), General Recommendations Nos. 19 and 20, Eleventh Session, in Document A/47/38 (1992).

[42] United Nations Commission on Human Rights, Convention on the Rights of the Child, 46th Session, E/CN.4/RES/1990/74 (March 7, 1990).

[43] United Nations General Assembly, Optional Protocol to the Convention on the Rights of the Child on the Sale of Children, Child Prostitution and Child Pornography, A/RES/54/263 (March 16, 2001).

[44] Council of Europe, Convention on Action Against Trafficking in Human Beings.

[45] Association of Southeast Asian Nations (ASEAN), Convention Against Trafficking in Persons, Especially Women and Children (Kuala Lumpur, November 21, 2015).

[46] *Rantsev v. Cyprus and Russia*, App. No. 25965/04, European Court of Human Rights (ECHR), January 7, 2010; *Chowdury v. Greece*, ECHR, January 7, 2010.

[47] ASEAN, ASEAN Human Rights Declaration (November 18, 2012).

first steps in addressing human trafficking and incorporated for the first-time specific regulations against trafficking in human beings. The Protocol has had a significant impact and has been ratified by nearly every country in the world. Alongside the UNTOC, it has become a crucial tool for national law enforcement and even the judiciary, leading to the creation of specialized units dedicated to fighting this horrific crime.

Yet challenges remain, particularly due to the Protocol's broad definition of human trafficking. The definition has led to some difficulties, especially regarding issues like dual criminalization in extradition treaties. Despite these challenges, the Protocol outlines a comprehensive set of goals and practical steps to address human trafficking effectively. These measures include prevention, victim protection, compensation, and punishing perpetrators, though the measures are presented in a wide-ranging and flexible way to the state's parties.

One notable deficiency within the Protocol is the absence of a mandatory reflection period, a measure commonly utilized in several countries in their efforts against human trafficking[48].Victims of human trafficking often find themselves in precarious situations in foreign countries, where the assurance that they will not be swiftly deported to their countries of origin is crucial for encouraging their cooperation. Establishing trust and confidence with victims assumes a critical role in both investigative procedures and preventive endeavors.

Another important point is the need to take a human rights-based approach. Victims should be seen as rights-holders, and the state is the duty-bearer, responsible for ensuring that victims' rights are protected and upheld. This perspective is key to creating lasting solutions, not just temporary fixes[49]. A human rights-based approach is crucial for fully tackling the complexity of human trafficking and ensuring that the rights of victims are at the forefront of every effort.

---

[48] Council of Europe, Convention Against Trafficking in Human Beings, art. 13.

[49]OHCHR et al., Joint UN Commentary on the EU Directive: A Human Rights Based Approach (2011), 25.

3.2.1. The Role of Companies in the Fight against the Trafficking of Human Beings

We usually forget the major role that legal persons can play in combating trafficking in human beings, despite studies showing the importance of companies in this globalized crime. According to a report prepared by the Ashridge Centre for Business and Sustainability at Hult International Business School and the Ethical Trading Initiative, 77 per cent of companies think that there is likely to believe that modern slavery occurs in their supply chain[50]. As we saw earlier, Article 10 of the UNTOC requires each State Party to establish the liability of legal persons for involvement in serious crimes, including trafficking in human beings. This liability can be criminal, civil, or administrative, but it should effectively address the crime.

In a similar vein, the Council of Europe Convention on Action against Trafficking in Human Beings, and the Directive 2011/36[51], also highlight the importance of holding legal persons accountable, taking into account that businesses must play a key role in preventing and addressing human trafficking.

Turning to national legislation, noteworthy examples include the UK Modern Slavery Act of 2015[52] and the California Transparency in Supply Chains Act of 2010[53]. These acts impose obligations on large corporations to prevent human trafficking in their supply chains, representing significant progress in the fight against trafficking of human beings for labor purposes. For instance, Section 54 of the UK Modern Slavery Act mandates companies with an annual turnover exceeding £36m[54] to publish an annual slavery and human trafficking statement, providing detailed information on organizational structure, training, policies, identified risks, and due diligence processes.

The California Act, targeting companies with a global turnover of over $100 million, requires public disclosure on company websites regarding

---

[50] Hult International Business School and The Ethical Trading Initiative, Corporate Leadership on Modern Slavery (November 2016), 7.

[51] European Union, Directive 2011/36/EU of the European Parliament and of the Council of April 5, 2011, on Preventing and Combating Trafficking in Human Beings and Protecting Its Victims, and Replacing Council Framework Decision 2002/629/JHA, Official Journal of the European Union L 101 (April 15, 2011): 1–11.

[52] United Kingdom, Modern Slavery Act *2015*, accessed September 11, 2024, https://www.legislation.gov.uk/ukpga/2015/30.

[53] California Department of Justice, California Transparency in Supply Chains Act, accessed November 24, 2024, https://oag.ca.gov/SB657.

[54] United Kingdom, Modern Slavery Act 2015, sec. 2(1).

specific activities to detect and prevent forced labor and human trafficking in supply chains. Failure to implement effective internal controls and due diligence programs may render companies criminally responsible in multiple states. We cannot demonstrate concrete data on how corporations are used to commit modern slavery, but it is clear that trafficking in human beings, by its very nature, it is often committed within company's activities and there are companies that are most at risk, such as industries involving agriculture, migrant workers, or seasonal product cycles. Therefore, trafficking poses a liability for all companies, potentially moral, civil, administrative, or even criminal depending on the jurisdiction. For this reason, companies should be aware of the responsibility that they have in the fight against human trafficking and the serious consequences for them if their employers or their managers are involved in this type of crime. Apart from punishment, they would suffer a huge non-material damage because of the process. Despite these regulations, cases against corporations remain infrequent. Several challenges, such as the extraterritorial application of corporate criminal liability, evidentiary issues, and complexities arising from subcontracting with intricate corporate structures, hinder successful prosecution.

Human trafficking, a form of transnational organized crime, involves the displacement of people across borders, making companies susceptible to involvement in recruitment, transportation, or exploitation. The three main stages - recruitment, transition, and exploitation - expose companies to specific legal and reputational risks.

a. First Stage: Recruitment.

Recruitment, often facilitated through social networks and false online job postings, poses a significant risk for companies. To combat this, effective Trafficking in Human Beings detection systems must be implemented, particularly in companies operating online, including porn websites. Other, such as private employment agencies also play a crucial role, necessitating coordinated efforts to regulate, license, and monitor these entities. The initial stage of the trafficking process consists of the recruitment. It can be done by several means, and it depends on the purpose of the offence. However, there are usual forms of recruitment, both for labor exploitation and in sexual exploitation.

Social networks play a fundamental role in the recruitment phase and for that reason it is extremely important to implement in those companies' effective detections systems. It appears that 89% of youth aged 12–17 enjoy chatting online[55]: class-mates, chat rooms or web nets. These are perfect points for traffickers, who use false identities to lure potential victims to a meeting.

With regard also to the Internet, it is common to make use of false jobs advertisements placed on it. It seems to be difficult to detect that type of simulated jobs, but it is also possible to implement different channels for identifying presumed traffickers. The patterns of the trafficking process are always similar. The companies that operate on the Internet should be on the lookout for signs of trafficking.

Nevertheless, it cannot be ignored that the identification on the Internet is very difficult[56]. The anonymity and mass audience of online services increases both the discretion and profitability of the services but complicates the fight against the recruitment. For that reason, the companies that operate on the Internet should increase the delivery of information to users in relation to this crime. Companies should highlight the risk of being victim of trafficking and they should explain the traditional methods used by traffickers. Furthermore, companies should also provide users with direct contacts of the company specialized in the fight against human trafficking, representing intermediaries between users and police authorities.

b. Second Stage: Transition.

Transportation of victims during the transition stage requires measures to prevent the crime within key sectors, such as shipping, hospitality, and transportation services. Shipping companies must be vigilant, as they can be held responsible if traffickers misuse their services.

c. Third Stage: Exploitation.

Exploitation, the final stage of human trafficking, poses the highest risk for companies. Sectors with a heightened risk include agriculture, construction, electronics, fishing, healthcare, hospitality, mining, tourism, and textile manufacturing. Companies operating in these sectors should establish robust trafficking in human beings detection mechanisms.

In order to eradicate human trafficking in companies, it is essential to have a holistic response involving multiple stakeholders. Small, medium, and large

---

[55] Susannah Fox, "Fact Sheet: Teens and Young Adults, Social Media, Online Health Resources," accessed September 11, 2024, https://susannahfox.com/research/differences-by-age-group/.

[56] Europol, "Migrant Smugglers and Human Traffickers: More Digital and Highly Adaptable," accessed September 11, 2024, https://www.europol.europa.eu/media-press/newsroom/news/migrant-smugglers-and-human-traffickers-more-digital-and-highly-adaptable.

companies should actively participate in the fight against human trafficking, disrupting traffickers' use of corporations for their criminal activities. Companies aware of the risks have initiated commendable efforts, such as Truckers Against Human Trafficking[57] and the European Alliance Bankers against Trafficking in Human Beings[58].

With globalization, companies must comply with international standards. While there is a growing trend towards corporate criminal liability worldwide, many companies remain unaware of the risks they face without implementing effective anti-trafficking measures. It is the responsibility of all stakeholders, including judicial authorities, policymakers, the press, and the public, to raise awareness about the necessity of implementing due diligence programs, internal controls, and specific policies to address human trafficking risks and prevent labor exploitation. Only through collective efforts can we combat human trafficking comprehensively.

3.3. Second Protocol: Protocol against Migrant Smuggling

On 15 November 2000, the General Assembly adopted the Protocol against the Smuggling of Migrants by Land, Sea, and Air, complementing the UNTOC. This protocol has been ratified by 126 countries[59]; It responds to the growing global challenge of irregular migration and organized smuggling networks.

Globalization has led to an unprecedented level of interconnectedness worldwide. Millions of people live outside their own countries, and increasing people are on the move, whether fleeing poverty, war or, in short, in search of a better life. However, the supply of regular immigration does not match the demand, which is where smuggling networks intervene. It is a highly controversial issue, with debates about its causes, characteristics and the response that should be given. For many countries, the fight against migrant smuggling is not a priority, and its seriousness is minimized despite the tragic cost of human lives it entails. However, the phenomenon is unstoppable and

---

[57] Truckers Against Trafficking (TAT), "TAT Mobilises Key Industries and Agencies to Combat Human Trafficking," accessed November 7, 2024, https://tatnonprofit.org/.

[58] Reuters, "European Banks Join Drive to Combat Human Trafficking Using Data," accessed November 7, 2024, https://www.reuters.com/article/world/european-banks-join-drive-to-combat-human-trafficking-using-data-idUSKBN0OP1RM/.

[59] United Nations, "Treaty Collection," accessed November 11, 2024, https://treaties.un.org/pages/ViewDetails.aspx?src=TREATY&mtdsg_no=XVIII-12&chapter=18&clang=en.

needs to be tackled in a courageous and determined manner with respect for human rights. States should encourage regular migration, increase the supply, assist countries of origin, promote international cooperation on criminal matters, and provide information about travel risks and the conditions and abuses perpetrated by migrant smugglers. Above all, they should seek common responses. Although such responses may seem difficult to achieve, the Palermo Protocol could serve as a first step on this journey.

Notably, not all migrants are victims of smuggling, but a significant number fall prey to this criminal enterprise. Tragically, the pursuit of financial gains by the smugglers often results in the loss of human lives. Thousands of migrants die each year due to accidents, inhospitable terrains, harsh weather conditions, or even deliberate killings. Smugglers, driven by profit motives, frequently neglect the safety and well-being of those they transport. The Mediterranean routes alone witnessed the smuggling of approximately 375,000 people annually into Europe and 735,000 to 820,000 people into North America[60]. From neighboring countries to Thailand: 550,000 (in 2019); 162,000 from South-West Asia to Turkey; and 480,000 from Sub-Saharan Africa to North Africa. The economic dimension of migrant smuggling is highly significant, according to the first Global Study on Smuggling of Migrants [61] that at least 2.5 million migrants were smuggled, generating returns of €5.5 to 7 billion[62]. Tragically, thousands of migrants lose their lives each year due to accidents, inhospitable terrains, harsh weather conditions, or even deliberate killings, as smugglers prioritize financial gains over the safety of those they transport. Migrants who are smuggled are not only subjected to perilous conditions but are also vulnerable to various other crimes, including violations, extortions, and trafficking in human beings.

The challenges of complying with administrative requirements set by states or groups of states often force individuals to seek alternative, often irregular, means of migration. This is where migrant smugglers play a role, providing pathways for those facing difficulties in navigating the regulated immigration policies. On many occasions, smugglers deceive them by not telling them the risks they will carry during the trip or even lying to them. Nevertheless, despite the current and potential magnitude and consequences of this phenomenon, combating the smuggling of migrants has not been a

[60] United Nations Office on Drugs and Crime (UNODC), *Global Study on Smuggling of Migrants* (New York: UNODC, 2018), accessed September 11, 2024, https://www.unodc.org/unodc/en/data-and-analysis/som-observatory.html.
[61] UNODC, *Global Study on Smuggling of Migrants*, 22.
[62] Ibid., 22.

priority in many countries, remaining primarily overlooked and poorly understood[63]; smuggling of migrants often shares the same characteristics as other transnational organized markets. Smugglers advertise their businesses where migrants can be easily reached. The demands are determined by the limited channels for regular migration and their costs that, in most cases, migrants cannot afford. Tragically, demand for smuggling services is exceptionally high among refugees[64].

People leave their countries of origin for various reasons, ranging from seeking improved living conditions to escaping conflicts, natural disasters, false promises of a better life posed by smugglers, or a lack of opportunities. Individuals may cross international borders without the requisite travel documents, either independently or with the assistance of professional smugglers. Such crossing can occur[65]:

Off the beaten path: Away from regular border points, through green (land/woods), blue (river/lake/sea), or white (onboard flying object) borders. Concealed crossing: This occurs via regular border crossings but is concealed in various modes of transportation such as trucks, cars, ships, trains, or aircraft.

Legal deception at the border:

Some migrants, cross borders using seemingly legal means that involve deception such as:

1. Document fraud: Using either falsified or stolen documents.
2. Visa manipulation: Presenting a regular document featuring a forged/falsified visa.
3. Violating visa conditions: Host countries typically issue various types of visas, each specifying entry and stay conditions for distinct purposes. Violating these conditions renders a person illegal or undocumented, either by:
4. Overstaying: Exceeding the permitted period granted upon entry.

Violating entry conditions: Engaging in activities inconsistent with the visa's intended purpose (e.g., using a student visa for employment, false marriages, false family reunions, etc.).

---

[63]Andreas Schloenhardt and J. E. Dale, "Twelve Years On: Revisiting the UN Protocol Against the Smuggling of Migrants by Land, Sea and Air," *Zeitschrift für Öffentliches Recht* 67 (2012): 129–156, at 133.

[64]UNODC, *Global Study on Smuggling of Migrants*, 6.

[65] International Organization for Migration (IOM), *World Migration Report 2022*, accessed November 7, 2024, https://worldmigrationreport.iom.int/wmr-2022-interactive/.

Throughout the journey, smuggled individuals often face heightened risks due to the neglect or harsh conditions of the trip. Despite the tragic numbers as consequence of the smuggling of migrants, before establishing the Protocol against the smuggling of migrants, there were significant gaps in the institutional framework of cooperation and domestic laws. These gaps prevented states from collaborating to prohibit and prosecute smugglers[66]. Additionally, in many countries, migrant smuggling was not considered a crime. The Protocol addresses these shortcomings, representing a ground-breaking and distinctive framework. It introduces, for the first time, an internationally recognized concept of migrant smuggling, mandates its prosecution, and functions as a tool for fostering international cooperation. The Protocol purposes are both the prevention and the combat of migrant smuggling. Beyond enforcement, it fosters cooperation among states parties, emphasizing the delicate balance between these objectives and protecting the rights of the very individuals caught in the web of this illicit trade. The Protocol aims to safeguard the rights of smuggled migrants, while highlighting the challenges presented by the transnational nature.

The Protocol defines smuggling of migrants as the intentional procurement, for financial or material gain, of the illegal entry of a person into a State Party where the individual is neither a national nor a permanent resident[67].

The Smuggling Protocol focuses on the prevention, investigation, and prosecution of the smuggling of migrants involving organized criminal groups, and it underscores the imperative of protecting the rights of every citizen smuggled[68].

States parties are obligated to criminalize intentional acts associated with migrant smuggling[69]. This obligation includes producing fraudulent documents and facilitating illegal stays for non-nationals. The Protocol delineates measures against accomplices and those organizing or directing such offenses. The Protocol states to criminalize the smuggling of migrants where previously the offenses were limited or non-existent[70].

Concerning consent in migration, the definition of migrant smuggling may imply that those being smuggled are willing participants. Nevertheless,

---

[66] UNODC, Palermo Convention: Twelve Years Later, 133.
[67] UNODC, Palermo Convention: Twelve Years Later, art. 3, 133.
[68] UNODC, Global Study on Smuggling of Migrants, 6.
[69] Protocol Against the Smuggling of Migrants by Land, Sea and Air, art. 6.
[70] Andreas Schloenhardt, "Twelve Years Later," in *Palermo Convention: Retrospectives and Prospects*, 139.

consent is only sometimes evident, particularly when coercion or unclear grounds for consenting to the smuggling process exist[71]. Consequently, consent alone cannot reliably distinguish between someone being smuggled and someone being trafficked. This complexity poses challenges in differentiating between the two phenomena during transit, especially when individuals have not yet been exploited, highlighting the crucial distinction between these two criminal activities.

Acknowledging the unique challenges of maritime routes, the Protocol outlines special provisions for cooperation among states parties to prevent and suppress smuggling by sea due to the pronounced risks involved[72]. These provisions include authorization to board, search, and respond appropriately against vessels raising suspicion. Since the promulgation of the Protocol, there have been debates about whether it creates a new right of action regarding stateless smuggling vessels on the high sea beyond the powers permitted under the Convention on the Law of the Sea (UNCLOS)[73] right of visit. Nevertheless, neither customary international law nor the UNCLOS provides enforcement jurisdiction over stateless vessels, and the question remains debatable[74]. Nevertheless, a State Party is permitted to board and search a vessel if there are reasonable grounds to suspect its involvement in smuggling migrants by sea, especially if the vessel is without nationality or can be considered akin to a stateless vessel[75]. If evidence substantiating the suspicion is discovered, the State Party must take suitable actions in line with domestic and international law. States have utilized this provision to legitimize high-seas enforcement actions against stateless smuggling vessels.

Consequently, it becomes essential to clarify the specific meaning and scope of the term "appropriate measures" as outlined in the Migrant Smuggling Protocol[76]. Moreover, states parties are encouraged to foster a collaborative environment, with an exchange of information, reinforcement of border controls, document security measures, training initiatives, and public awareness campaigns to prevent and combat migrant smuggling

---

71 A. Aljehani, "The Legal Definition of the Smuggling of Migrants in Light of the Provisions of the Migrant Smuggling Protocol," *The Journal of Criminal Law* 79, no. 2 (2015): 130–131

72 Protocol Against the Smuggling of Migrants by Land, Sea and Air, arts. 7–9.

73 United Nations Convention on the Law of the Sea, opened for signature December 10, 1982, 1833 U.N.T.S. 397 (entered into force November 16, 1994).

74 Thea Coventry, "Seizing Stateless Smuggling Vessels on the Mediterranean High Seas," *Leiden Journal of International Law* 36, no. 4 (2023): 946.

75 United Nations, United Nations Convention Against Transnational Organized Crime *(UNTOC)*, art. 8.7.

76 Coventry, "Seizing Stateless Smuggling Vessels," 950.

comprehensively. The Protocol places emphasis on protecting the rights of individuals subjected to smuggling, encompassing safeguards against violence and provisions for assistance in cases where their lives or safety are endangered, as well as provisions to facilitate the orderly return of smuggled migrants to their home countries, with states parties outlined specific responsibilities in the process. The Protocol on Migrant Smuggling has garnered widespread support from member states, marking a success in establishing a universally recognized definition of migrant smuggling and compelling states parties to criminalize this activity. It introduces a humanitarian perspective, considering the needs of smuggled individuals and outlining clear obligations for states. Despite these achievements, joining the UNTOC it is a prerequisite for its application, posing challenges to prosecution due to the requirement to demonstrate involvement by an organized crime entity. Concerning the links between smuggling networks and other criminal markets, although it might seem such links are not the norm, in reality there is a clear connection between migrant smuggling and corruption at many levels and along the route[77].

The mandate for a group structure of three individuals further complicates investigations under the Migrant Smuggling Protocol. Additionally, this Protocol used by some countries to seize stateless vessels[78], needs more clarity, and stands outside the provisions of the United Nations Convention on the law of the Sea[79]. It is essential to clarify this article to strengthen protections for migrants and asylum seekers[80].

The Protocol against migrant smuggling has contributed to being the first international instrument to define and criminalize the smuggling of persons, to promote international cooperation and to protect the rights of persons smuggled. The development of a common framework is essential to encourage and support cooperation. Although there is still reluctance on the part of many states to ratify it, it has gained in importance over time. The Protocol on migrant smuggling calls explicitly for the non-criminalization of migrants and advises states to report on criminal business and immigration officials to be aware of migrants' rights, such as the right to non-refoulement. It must be stressed that the response can never be exclusively criminal and it cannot be

---

[77] UNODC, *Global Study on Smuggling of Migrants* (2018), 52.
[78] United Nations, Protocol Against the Illicit Manufacturing of and Trafficking in Firearms, Their Parts and Components and Ammunition, Supplementing the UNTOC, art. 8.7.
[79] United Nations Convention on the Law of the Sea, 1833 U.N.T.S. 397.
[80] Coventry, "Seizing Stateless Smuggling Vessels," 946.

ignored that refugees themselves are forced to turn to smugglers for lack of alternative mechanisms.

Despite all this, the response to immigration remains, for the most part, strictly an internal matter for states. The immigration policy remains, in most cases, within the domestic borders. An exception can be found in the EU framework. In recent years, the EU has moved towards a standard policy about immigration matters and about migrant smuggling[81]. In recent years, the European Union has progressively shifted towards formulating a unified immigration policy. This evolution is manifest in key policy initiatives, commencing with adopting the Global Approach to Migration and Mobility[82] (GAMM) in 2011. Subsequently, in May 2015[83], the European Commission published the European Agenda on Migration, a response to the escalating irregular immigration crisis, notably in the Mediterranean region. The year 2020 witnessed a pivotal development with the introduction of the new Pact on Migration and Asylum by the European Commission[84]. On 10 April 2024, the European Parliament voted in favor of the new rules on migration. Moreover, the Commission has also launched a Call to Action for a Global Alliance to Counter Migrant Smuggling[85].

Despite this advance in common politics, it remains a material heavily used for electoral purposes in the various countries of the European Union, challenging a common response. Their main overseas counterparts: the US, Canada, and Australia take their political action on immigration entirely on the national level.

A narrow focus on combating migrant smuggling undermines our ability to effectively address this complex issue. Migrants, often forced to pay exorbitant fees, endure perilous journeys fraught with danger and deception. They are misled about the route's conditions and destination country. Only

---

[81] European Commission, "Managing Migration Better in All Aspects: A European Agenda on Migration," accessed November 24, 2024, https://ec.europa.eu/commission/presscorner/detail/en/ip_15_4956.

[82] European Commission, "Global Approach to Migration and Mobility," accessed November 22, 2024, https://home-affairs.ec.europa.eu/networks/european-migration-network-emn/emn-asylum-and-migration-glossary/glossary/global-approach-migration-and-mobility-gamm_en.

[83] European Union, *A European Agenda on Migration*, Communication from the Commission, COM (2015) 0240.

[84] European Commission, "Managing Migration Responsibly," accessed September 11, 2024, https://commission.europa.eu/strategy-and-policy/priorities-2019-2024/story-von-der-leyen-commission/managing-migration-responsibly_en.

[85] European Commission, Directorate-General for Migration and Home Affairs, *Call to Action on a Global Alliance to Counter Migrant Smuggling* (Luxembourg: Publications Office of the European Union, 2024).

through a concerted, international effort - comprising information sharing, expanding legal migration opportunities, and fostering cooperation against criminal networks - can we reduce the number of migrants falling prey to smugglers. This effort requires a human rights-based approach. Merely tightening border controls and embracing protectionist measures is not an adequate response. Instead, we must prioritize the dignity and safety of migrants, offering them viable alternatives through legal migration pathways.

Additionally, fostering collaboration among states is crucial for dismantling smuggling operations and holding perpetrators accountable. However, while this courageous and decisive common response is being addressed, the Palermo Protocol laid the foundations for cooperation in the fight against trafficking in human beings. It is essential to get more states to ratify it, make progress in monitoring compliance with the Protocol through the monitoring mechanism, clarify the use of seizure of vessels at sea in article 8.7, and progress on the rights of migrants and refugees.

Migrant smuggling holds global significance, yet further efforts are needed for broader ratification by countries worldwide. Despite existing barriers hindering some nations from signing agreements, the escalating challenge of migrant smuggling is undeniable. Therefore, a coordinated, comprehensive response involving both origin and destination countries is imperative.

By adopting a comprehensive strategy that addresses the underlying drivers of migration while upholding human rights, we can effectively combat migrant smuggling and create a more just and humane system for all.

3.4. Third Protocol: Firearms Protocol

On May 31, 2001, the United Nations General Assembly adopted the Firearms Protocol, which entered into force on July 3, 2005. The Protocol provides a framework for countries to control and monitor the legal trade of firearms, prevent their diversion into illegal markets, and support the investigation and prosecution of related crimes - all without interfering with lawful arms transfers.

Although it has not been ratified as widely as the Protocol against Human Trafficking or the Protocol against Migrant Smuggling, the Firearms Protocol still holds considerable relevance. To date, it has been signed by 52 countries and ratified by 123[86]. However, in academic circles, it has received less attention than its counterparts in the other two protocols and is generally less recognized. Nevertheless, it addresses a critically important issue that affects countries worldwide. Global statistics on violent crimes involving firearms are alarming, with approximately 700 people dying from firearm use every day[87]. Moreover, there were an estimated 857 million civilian-held firearms worldwide by the end of 2017, with only 100 million registered[88]. This indicates that most firearms globally are privately owned, making their documentation particularly challenging.

The proliferation of uncontrolled firearms among civilians clearly leads to increased violence within societies, with over 40 percent of crimes involving firearms.[89] Furthermore, the spread of small arms poses serious risks to the stability of states, citizen safety, democratic institutions, and global security. It fuels rising crime rates, strengthens organized crime groups, and even empowers terrorist organizations. When weapons circulate without proper regulation, they also intensify armed conflicts and contribute to the recruitment of children as soldiers.

Small arms have had devastating effects in many countries, particularly in Africa. In other regions, such as Central and South America, the illegal flow of weapons - particularly from the United States to Mexico - has become a growing concern. Although the Firearms Protocol may not be as widely recognized as the other two protocols, its importance cannot be overstated. It tackles a key issue for global peace and security.

Data from countries like South Africa show that reducing and controlling firearms can lead to a significant drop in violent crime. Recognizing this, the United Nations made reducing arms flows a key part of Goal 16 of the 2030 Agenda for Sustainable Development[90].

In addition to the Arms Protocol, several other legal instruments play a key role in addressing the illicit trade in firearms. One such instrument is the United Nations Register of Conventional Arms, which seeks to promote

---

86 United Nations, "Treaty Collection," accessed September 30, 2024, https://treaties.un.org/Pages/ViewDetails.aspx?src=TREATY&mtdsg_no=XVIII-12-c&chapter=18&clang=_en.

87 Small Arms Survey, "Russia's War: Weighing the Human Cost in Ukraine," accessed September 11, 2024, https://www.smallarmssurvey.org/taxonomy/term/182.

88 Aaron Karp, *Estimating Global Civilian-Held Firearms Numbers* (Geneva: Small Arms Survey, June 2018), 3.

89 Gergely Hideg and Anna Alvazzi del Frate, *Still Not There: Global Violent Deaths Scenarios, 2019–2030*, Small Arms Survey Briefing Paper (February 2021), 3.

90 United Nations General Assembly, Transforming Our World: The 2030 Agenda for Sustainable Development, A/RES/70/1 (October 21, 2015).

transparency in the arms trade, build trust among states, and contribute to conflict prevention.

The Program of Action to Prevent, Combat, and Eradicate the Illicit Trade in Small Arms and Light Weapons in Its Aspects [91], adopted in 2001, provides a comprehensive and universal framework for international efforts against the illicit trade in small arms and light weapons.

The International Tracing Instrument (ITI), established in 2006 through a Franco-Swiss initiative, enables states to promptly and reliably identify and trace illicit small arms and light weapons. The Arms Trade Treaty (ATT[92]), adopted in 2013, represents the first global, legally binding instrument designed to regulate the trade in conventional arms and eliminate their illicit trade. The International Action Network on Small Arms (IANSA[93]) is a global movement that unites hundreds of organizations working to stop gun violence.

Gun violence is a matter of universal concern, with consequences ranging from physical injuries to victims to the less visible yet equally dramatic economic and emotional impact on victims. Civil wars and regional/international conflicts have been fueled by the existence of small arms, exacerbating violence against women and girls who are often direct victims of such conflicts.

The Firearms Protocol aims to promote and strengthen international cooperation, developing cohesive mechanisms to prevent, combat, and eradicate the illicit manufacturing and trafficking of firearms, their parts, components, and ammunition. By ratifying or acceding to the Firearms Protocol, states commit to adopting and implementing a series of crime-control measures, including:

a. Criminalizing the illicit manufacturing and trafficking of firearms
b. Implementing effective control and security measures to prevent theft and diversion of firearms into illicit channels;
c. Establishing a system of government authorizations or licensing to regulate legitimate manufacturing and trafficking of firearms;
d. Ensuring proper marking, recording, and tracing of firearms, along with effective international cooperation for these purposes.

---

[91] United Nations Office for Disarmament Affairs (UNODA), established January 1998 as part of the Secretary-General's reform program (A/51/950).

[92] United Nations General Assembly, Arms Trade Treaty, Resolution 67/234B (April 2, 2013).

[93] International Action Network on Small Arms (IANSA), accessed September 11, 2024, https://iansa.org/.

Central to the Firearms Protocol is the precise definition of key terms such as "firearm," "parts and components," and "ammunition." A firearm, as stipulated in the Protocol, refers to any portable barreled weapon designed for projectile expulsion through explosive action, excluding antique firearms or post-1899 replicas. Understanding these definitions is pivotal, as they form the basis for identifying illicit activities such as manufacturing and trafficking[94]. A key part of the Firearms Protocol is the requirement for countries to make certain firearms-related crimes punishable by law. This includes illegal manufacturing, trafficking, and tampering with firearm markings. By doing so, states parties are expected to create strong legal tools to fight organized crime groups involved in the illegal arms trade. The Protocol also encourages the confiscation and seizure of illegal firearms, ammunition, and parts, helping to prevent them from reaching the wrong hands. In addition, it recommends that countries allow for the forfeiture of these weapons even if there is no criminal conviction, as a way to reduce risks further and prevent future crimes.

The Firearms Protocol emphasizes the importance of preventive measures to curb illicit firearms activities. States parties are required to maintain records of information in relation to firearms for a minimum of ten years, enabling the tracing of illicit firearms and related items. Furthermore, strict marking requirements at the manufacturing, import, and civilian transfer stages ensure effective identification and tracking of firearms, enhancing accountability and transparency in the supply chain.

To prevent reactivated weapons from re-entering circulation, the Protocol sets stringent guidelines for rendering them permanently inoperable. Verification by competent authorities is essential to certify the deactivation process. Additionally, states must establish robust systems for the licensing and authorization of firearms' export, import, and transit, ensuring stringent oversight and control over cross-border movements. If other forms of disposal are selected over destruction then, the firearms must be marked and the method of disposal recorded. Marking and record-keeping are fundamental steps in combating illicit trafficking. However, these measures alone are insufficient and must be reinforced through close cooperation between states.[95]

Enhancing security measures, particularly at borders, is highlighted in the Protocol to prevent illicit firearms from entering or leaving a country undetected. Cooperation among states parties is crucial, with provisions for

---

[94] UNODC, *Technical Guide to the Implementation of the Protocol Against the Illicit Manufacturing of and Trafficking in Firearms* (New York: United Nations, 2011), 4.

[95] Organization for Security and Co-operation in Europe (OSCE), *Handbook of Best Practices on Small Arms and Light Weapons* (Vienna, 2003), 2.

the exchange of information on producers, dealers, and criminal groups involved in firearms trafficking. This information sharing extends to scientific and technological advancements, aiding law enforcement agencies in their efforts to combat illicit activities.

The Firearms Protocol also highlights the importance of the role of the brokers to control the illicit flows of arms has been practically a new issue since very few countries imposed those controls by the time of the Protocol[96]. Recognizing the key role of brokers in firearms transactions, the Protocol urges states to establish regulatory frameworks encompassing registration, licensing, and disclosure requirements for brokers. This ensures greater transparency and accountability in firearms transactions, mitigating the risk of illicit trade. Brokering controls are essential to allow states to identify the activities of persons who operate in grey areas or in the illegal sector[97].

The proliferation and increasing accessibility of arms among civilian populations lead to alarming rises in mortality rates, criminal activities, and violence. This unchecked spread of weaponry exacerbates societal instability and threatens national and regional stability. Comprehensive efforts must be made to mitigate these risks and foster a global environment that prioritizes safety and peace.

Despite the significant legislative progress achieved through the arms protocol and the other legislative initiatives, it remains crucial to encourage more countries to adopt and implement the Firearms Protocol. Although the protocol has introduced important innovations, many countries still exhibit reluctance to sign it. To address this, robust awareness-raising campaigns and sustained international pressure are essential to confront the pervasive challenge posed by the arms trade.

---

[96] OSCE, *Handbook of Best Practices*, 4.
[97] Ibid., 4.

Chapter 4

Analysis of Traditional Transnational Crimes

4.1. Corruption

Corruption should not be seen as an isolated offense; it acts as a gateway for the expansion of other crimes including organized crime and transnational organized crime.

Broadly defined as the misuse of power for private gain[1], or, as one of the co-authors (Prof. Anis) has termed it for over two decades—a seemingly victimless, hidden trade-off between influence and gain[2], corruption challenges the principles of legal governance, delegation, and societal equity. An influence can be political or – as often translated - related to the public office or corporate position, while the gain can be private or corporate, commercial, or political. Corruption undermines public trust in institutions and weakens people's belief in the political system, while also draining public resources that should be used for legitimate purposes.

The impact of corruption is profound and widespread, with the potential to weaken democratic systems, erode institutional trust, foster societal insecurity, and fuel extremist political movements that claim to fight corruption. Despite governments' promises to address corruption, the reality is that it has expanded with globalization, transforming it into a global issue rather than one confined to particular states. The consequences ripple through societies and economies, often leading to secondary crimes such as economic offenses and money laundering.

Attacking corruption is no longer just a matter for individual countries; it requires international cooperation. While each state is primarily responsible for addressing corruption within its borders, the global nature of this threat necessitates a coordinated effort among nations.

---

[1] Susan Rose-Ackerman, "Corruption," in *Readings in Public Choice and Constitutional Political Economy*, eds. Charles K. Rowley and Friedrich G. Schneider (Boston, MA: Springer US, 2008), 551–566.

[2] Anis Bajrektarević, "Justice-Home Affairs Diplomacy – The Palermo Convention, 10 Years After," *Global Humanities International Research Journal* 3, no. 1 (2011).

The importance of the fight against corruption is acknowledged in General Assembly Resolution 54/128[3], where the ad hoc Committee, concurrently negotiating the Palermo Convention, was tasked with considering the need for a separate instrument to address corruption. Through extensive consultations, the Committee concluded that a distinct instrument was indeed required. This conclusion was subsequently communicated to the General Assembly, resulting in the adoption of UN General Assembly resolution 55/61[4]. This resolution mandated the creation of a separate instrument to combat corruption, alongside the establishment of an expert group tasked with formulating its terms of reference.

The Expert group assembled in Vienna in 2002, generating draft terms of reference subsequently transmitted to the General Assembly (GA) via the Commission on Crime Prevention and Criminal Justice[5] (CICP) and the Economic and Social Council (ECOSOC[6]). These terms of reference, adopted by the GA through resolution UN GA 56/260[7], provided crucial clarity on the subjects under negotiation. Presented during the second meeting of the Ad Hoc Committee, this key resolution set the stage for the resolution of myriad critical issues over seven sessions, culminating in the finalization of the United Nations Convention against Corruption (hereinafter, UNCAC or Mérida Convention)

Two particularly challenging matters dominated the discussions: first, the nuanced delineation of corruption itself—establishing the primary scope of the impending instrument (including considerations on the inclusion of private-sector corruption, among others); and second, the intricate political and legal ramifications of "grand corruption" cases involving high-ranking officials.

At that juncture, the Ad Hoc Committee along with the UNODC secretariat, orchestrated the conclusion of the Corruption Convention—an accomplishment that remains among the fastest in UN convention history. Despite its significance, the resulting instrument failed to address corruption within the private sector, making it a partial success at best. Influential

---

[3] United Nations General Assembly, Resolution Adopted by the General Assembly: A/RES/54/128, Action Against Corruption, 54th session, agenda item 107 (January 28, 2000).

[4] United Nations General Assembly, Resolution 55/61: An Effective International Legal Instrument Against Corruption, A/RES/55/61 (January 22, 2001).

[5] United Nations General Assembly, Resolution 1992/*1:* Establishment of the Commission on Crime Prevention and Criminal Justice (February 6, 1992).

[6] United Nations, "Economic and Social Council," accessed September 11, 2024, https://ecosoc.un.org/en.

[7] United Nations General Assembly, Terms of Reference for Negotiation of an International Legal Instrument Against Corruption (April 9, 2002).

countries were reluctant to adopt a unified approach to tackle public and private sector corruption within a single framework. As a result, member states were given concessions to speed up proceedings, but this led to a compromise, weakening the instrument and leaving it incomplete.

Corruption often operates in subtle ways, evading immediate detection. Behind closed doors, individuals in positions of power - whether in government or business - exploit their authority for personal or illicit gain. This hidden nature makes it challenging to uncover, requiring advanced investigative methods and a strong legal framework to prosecute. In many cases, no clear victim suffers immediate harm. Instead, the consequences of corruption are felt over time, gradually eroding public trust in institutions, distorting market processes, and deepening societal inequalities. Corruption involves the abuse of power for personal or illicit benefits, manifesting in forms like bribery, embezzlement, nepotism, and favoritism, all of which undermine fair competition, economic stability, and equal distribution of resources.

Efforts to combat corruption must go beyond legal frameworks and enforcement. They need to promote ethical leadership, transparency in decision-making, and empower civil society to hold authorities accountable. While the UNCAC lays down a necessary foundation, defining corruption more clearly would have been beneficial. A clearer definition would have minimized differences in how countries interpret and apply it, which even challenge international cooperation.

The UNCAC sets out the roles of public officials but leaves room for interpretation across different countries. This lack of a precise definition affects the consistency and effectiveness of its implementation. Nevertheless, the UNCAC stresses the need for strategies that enhance transparency. Key efforts focus on ensuring fair and transparent recruitment and promotion processes for civil servants, focusing on merit over nepotism[8]. It also encourages training programs to help officials understand corruption risks and foster an ethical culture within public institutions

Delving into the core of corruption, the Mérida Convention addresses the criminalization of corrupt acts, with a particular focus on activities involving public officials and private entities[9]. It explicitly condemns bribery, deeming it criminal to offer, give, solicit, or accept undue advantages. Additionally, it

[8] United Nations, United Nations Convention Against Corruption (UNCAC), arts. 5–14.
[9] Ibid., arts. 15–42.

censures the misappropriation of public funds, acts of embezzlement, and trading in influence.

Considering the transnational nature of corruption, UNCAC advocates for robust international collaboration[10]. States are urged to cooperate in investigations, prosecutions, and asset recovery endeavors. This includes measures to combat money laundering and illicit financial flows through cross-border cooperation. It provides a legal basis for mutual legal assistance in relation to the offenses foreseen by the Mérida Convention. If states were not bound by a mutual legal assistance treaty, the UNCAC could operate as a legal basis for affording such assistance. Therefore, states parties are encouraged to apply the provisions of the UNCAC in a complementary manner to existing mutual legal assistance treaties, requiring the designation of a central authority with the power to secure and execute mutual legal assistance requests or transmit them to the competent domestic authorities for execution[11].

A cornerstone of the Convention is the restitution of assets acquired through corrupt means. The UNCAC emphasizes the need for international cooperation to facilitate the recovery of illegally acquired gains. It provides channels for civil actions, compensation for damages and recognition of legitimate property rights.

Acknowledging the imperative for capacity-building, UNCAC promotes technical assistance and information exchange among states[12]. These initiatives aim to bolster the effective implementation of anti-corruption measures and foster enhanced cooperation in combating corruption.

Despite UNCAC's comprehensive provisions, challenges persist in its execution across numerous countries. Limitations such as inadequate coverage of specific offenses, inefficiencies in law enforcement, and deficiencies in existing legislation pose formidable obstacles. Many states struggle to fully implement the mandatory measures outlined in the UNCAC, underlining the need for sustained efforts and capacity-building initiatives. The year 2009 marked a major milestone with the establishment of the UNCAC's Implementation Review Mechanism at the Doha conference in Qatar.

---

[10] Ibid., arts. 43–50.
[11] Ibid., art. 46.
[12] Ibid., arts. 60–62.

Resolution 3/1 established this mechanism, with the UNODC entrusted as the secretariat[13].

The UNCAC Implementation Review Mechanism serves as a vital instrument to guide states parties in effectively implementing the Convention. Its key objectives include:

- Assisting states parties: Providing guidance and support to states parties in their comprehensive implementation of the Convention.
- Promoting Convention Objectives: Fostering transparency, integrity, and accountability in the fight against corruption.
- Informing the Conference of states parties: Offering insights into the measures taken by states parties and highlighting challenges encountered.
- Identifying Technical Assistance Needs: Facilitating the provision of technical assistance to states based on identified needs.
- Facilitating International Cooperation: Enhancing collaboration among states parties for more effective anti-corruption efforts.
- Sharing Successes and Challenges: Encouraging the exchange of best practices, challenges faced, and successes achieved in implementing the Convention.

The UNCAC review process, conducted through this Mechanism, has achieved notable successes. Participating states have responded proactively to the review findings, often implementing legislative reforms and policy improvements.

The Implementation Review Mechanism of the UNCAC aims to assess the successes, challenges, and needs for technical assistance in implementing each provision of the Convention. States parties embarking on legislative introductions or reforms must recognize the critical importance of conducting a thorough situational analysis, including consultations with stakeholders. Its continued evolution and effective implementation can lead to a more accountable future for public and private spheres.

Many completed reviews have suggested the adoption of suitable legislation and measures such as safeguarding whistle-blowers[14], enhancing

---

[13] United Nations Office on Drugs and Crime (UNODC), "Corruption and Economic Crime Branch," accessed November 24, 2024, https://www.unodc.org/corruption/en/cosp/conference/session3-resolutions.html.

[14] United Nations Office on Drugs and Crime (UNODC), *Resource Guide on Good Practices in the Protection of Reporting Persons* (New York: United Nations, 2015), 10.

existing protection schemes, and ensure that offenses under the UNCAC are explicitly covered within the framework of whistle-blower protection laws. These responsive actions have significantly contributed to the ongoing fight against corruption.

However, realizing the full potential of UNCAC demands concerted efforts from states to overcome implementation challenges and uphold the principles of transparency, accountability, and integrity. Through sustained collaboration, enhanced capacity-building, and diligent enforcement, states can forge a path toward a future marked by ethical governance and a resolute stance against corruption.

Corruption often poses a challenge for law enforcement, often remaining undetected due to the inherent benefit it provides to all parties involved in criminal activities. This underlines the need to establish mechanisms that facilitate reporting and safeguard whistle-blowers[15]. This includes guaranteeing confidentiality, instituting anonymous reporting mechanisms, and implementing witness protection schemes. Article 13(1) of the Convention thoroughly highlights the imperative for states to enact measures to ensure the freedom to investigate and disclose information relating to corruption. However, this freedom is limited, as there are limitations to freedom of expression itself. For such freedoms to be exercised, they must be clearly stipulated within the limits of the law. Any limitation must pursue a legitimate aim and respect the principles of neutrality and proportionality[16].

The Mérida Convention further identifies legitimate restrictions, which include safeguarding the rights and reputations of others, preserving national security or public order, and promoting public health. The concept of necessity dictates that any restriction imposed must be indispensable in achieving the legitimate goal, while proportionality necessitates that no alternative means are available to achieve the same objective with the least restrictive impact[17]. These practices reinforce the foundation for a transparent and accountable system, essential for combating corruption effectively.

Besides, individuals are entitled to protection against baseless accusations, as articulated in Article 33 of the Convention, which advocates for safeguarding those who make genuine and reasonable accusations against

---

[15] Council of Europe, Recommendation CM/Rec(2014)7 of the Committee of Ministers to Member States on the Protection of Whistleblowers, adopted April 30, 2014.

[16] United Nations Office on Drugs and Crime (UNODC), *Informer sur la corruption: Un Outil de Référence pour les Gouvernements et les Journalistes* (New York: United Nations, 2014), 42–43.

[17] UNODC, *Informer sur la corruption.*

others. In most cases, the disclosure of personal data should not be necessary to achieve the intended purpose[18].

A crucial aspect of the fight against corruption is, as already pointed out, whistleblowing. Since corruption can be embedded in institutions and governments, it is crucial that independent bodies provide unbiased analysis, highlighting and exposing cases of corruption. Transparency International has led this effort since 1995 through its annual Corruption Perceptions Index (CPI), reporting on corruption levels around the world[19]. This index meticulously assesses corruption levels in over 180 countries and territories worldwide. Over the span of 30 years, the CPI has emerged as the preeminent global indicator of corruption, providing invaluable insights into the state of corruption across the globe and its data are widely recognized.

Corruption, in essence, can be considered as theft from the impoverished. It represents a two-pronged assault on growth and prosperity, characterized not only by the misallocation of resources but also by the lasting repercussions of services not provided. This corruption's impact includes, for example, the failure to provide necessary educational materials, neglect in the construction of crucial infrastructure such as roads, and the denial of access to essential health care and education. Corruption perpetuates a cycle of deprivation that directly affects the most vulnerable populations and deprives them of fundamental rights and opportunities for advancement. However, the complexity of the fight against corruption must be acknowledged. The fight against corruption becomes tough when those responsible for tackling it are themselves implicated in corrupt practices. This underlines the indispensable role of the press, international organizations, and independent studies in exposing and shedding light on systemic problems in each state. The fight against corruption should stand as a top priority for every State party to the Convention. It is imperative to engage diverse sectors of society in this battle, with media playing a pivotal role in raising awareness and encouraging the reporting of corrupt activities.

The UNCAC, alongside the UNTOC, serves as essential instruments in the fight against corruption. Both Conventions provide concrete frameworks that steer and unify international efforts against corruption. Additionally, regional initiatives have been noteworthy, including the African Union

---

[18] United Nations Office of Drugs and Crime, *Resource Guide on Good Practices in the Protection of Reporting Persons*, 26.

[19] Transparency International, "Corruption Perceptions Index," accessed September 11, 2024, https://www.transparency.org/en/cpi/2022/index/esp.

Convention on Preventing and Combating Corruption[20], Civil Law Convention on Corruption[21], Criminal Law Convention on Corruption[22], Additional Protocol to the Criminal Law Convention on Corruption, Inter-American Convention Against Corruption[23], Convention on Combating Bribery of Foreign Public Officials in International Business Transactions[24], and the United Nations Declaration Against Corruption and Bribery in International Commercial Transactions[25].

Other sources, organizations, and studies on global corruption, notable entities include the Asian Development Bank[26], Office of Anticorruption and Integrity with its Annual Reports[27], GAN Risk & Compliance Portal[28], Group of States Against Corruption[29] (GRECO), Organization for Economic Co-operation and Development[30] (OECD) with its Country Reports on the Implementation of the OECD Anti-Bribery Convention, U4 Anti-Corruption Resource Centre[31], and the World Bank with its Worldwide Governance Indicators[32].

All these conventions signify recognition that effectively combating corruption and other transnational crimes requires synchronized and

---

[20] African Union, Convention on Preventing and Combating Corruption, adopted July 11, 2003, entered into force August 5, 2006 (Maputo, Mozambique).

[21] Council of Europe, Civil Law Convention on Corruption, ETS No. 174 (Strasbourg, November 4, 1999), entered into force November 1, 2003.

[22] Council of Europe, Criminal Law Convention on Corruption, ETS No. 173 (Strasbourg, January 27, 1999), entered into force July 1, 2002.

[23] Organization of American States (OAS), "Who We Are," accessed November 24, 2024, https://www.oas.org/en/about/who_we_are.asp.

[24] Organisation for Economic Co-operation and Development (OECD), *Convention on Combating Bribery of Foreign Public Officials in International Business Transactions* (Paris, November 21, 1997).

[25] United Nations General Assembly, *Action Against Corruption and Bribery in International Commercial Transactions*, A/RES/53/176 (January 25, 1999).

[26] Asian Development Bank, "Who We Are," accessed December 4, 2024, https://www.adb.org/who-we-are.

[27] Asian Development Bank, "Publications and Documents," accessed November 29, 2024, https://www.adb.org/documents/series/office-anticorruption-and-integrity-annual-report.

[28] GAN Integrity, "We Are GAN Integrity," accessed November 24, 2024, https://www.ganintegrity.com/about/.

[29] Council of Europe, Resolution (99) 5 Establishing the Group of States Against Corruption (GRECO), adopted May 1, 1999.

[30] Organisation for Economic Co-operation and Development (OECD), Convention on the Organisation for Economic Co-operation and Development (with Supplementary Protocols Nos. 1 and 2), Paris, December 14, 1960.

[31] U4 Anti-Corruption Resource Centre, "About Us," accessed November 30, 2024, https://www.u4.no/.

[32] World Bank Group, "Worldwide Governance Indicators," accessed November 24, 2024, https://www.worldbank.org/en/publication/worldwide-governance-indicators.

collaborative efforts at the international level, enhancing institutional capacities.

4.2. Terrorism

The English word terror literally means extreme fear. Thus, according to the Oxford dictionary, terrorism means: the use of violence for political, religious or ideological ends[33]. It is easy to linguistically define terrorism, but the real problem starts when terrorism as a phenomenon (including its range and scope) must be politically and legally determined and effectively defined.

Low or high scale atrocities, domestic violence, or terrorism. International terrorism, state-sponsored terrorism, special war, secession, and self-determination. Armed conflict, declaration of war; social unrest, proscribed organization and undermining the constitutional order, upheaval and revolutionary movement. All these terms, as such, are somehow defined at the national level, incorporated in, and treated by the national legislation. However, defining them in a more universal way, —by achieving broad international consensus on the scope, wording and definition- turns out to be a delicate and complex problem.

To address these complexities, the UNODC delineates in its Model Law[34] three distinct definitions of terrorist acts:

a. Variant 1: This definition characterizes a terrorist act as any action that qualifies as an offense under the scope and terminology specified in one of the treaties listed in the annex to the 1999 International Convention for the Suppression of the Financing of Terrorism[35]. This establishes a legal framework based on internationally recognized treaties, promoting clarity and consistency.
b. Variant 2: According to this definition, a terrorist act encompasses any offense that falls within the scope and definitions of specific international treaties on the matter[36].

---

[33] Oxford University Press, *A Dictionary of Law*, accessed November 24, 2024, https://www.oxfordreference.com/display/10.1093/acref/9780199551248.001.0001/acref-9780199551248-e-3951.

[34] United Nations, *Model Legislation on Money Laundering and Financing of Terrorism* (December 1, 2005).

[35] United Nations, *Model Legislation on Money Laundering*, art. 2.

[36] United Nations, Annex of International Conventions referenced in the Model Law on Terrorism:

This comprehensive list of treaties underscores the diverse nature of terrorist offenses recognized under international law.

c. Variant 3: The third definition states that a terrorist act is any act that is aimed at causing death or serious bodily injury to a civilian or any individual not actively participating in hostilities during an armed conflict. This definition places emphasis on the intent behind the act - specifically, it aims to intimidate a population or compel a government or international organization to take or refrain from taking specific actions, thereby highlighting the tactical nature of terrorist activities in the broader context of coercion and intimidation.

Together, these definitions provide crucial guidance for national legal frameworks in addressing terrorism and enhancing international collaboration in combating the financing of such illicit activities.

As defining terrorism in any particular case implies a political component, this very category becomes quite extensive and subject to different readings and understandings. Having permanent – primarily political – disputes over the category and scale of 'conflict,' the contemporary international community repeatedly failed over decades to agree upon a single and comprehensive but universal instrument determining, prescribing, and combating terrorism. Because of these mostly political and less legal implications, today we are confronted with two dozen international (universal and regional) instruments, which are good, but far from being standardized and harmonized.

Thus, the tentative political definition of (international) terrorism could be as follows: terrorism is the use of violence as a political means of pressuring the government and/or society into accepting a radical socio-political and/or socio-economic change (ideological or territorial). The word terrorist is

---

– Convention for the Suppression of Unlawful Seizure of Aircraft (1970);
– Convention for the Suppression of Unlawful Acts Against the Safety of Civil Aviation (1971);
– Convention on the Prevention and Punishment of Crimes Against Internationally Protected Persons, Including Diplomatic Agents (1973);
– International Convention Against the Taking of Hostages (1979);
– Convention on the Physical Protection of Nuclear Material (1980);
– Protocol for the Suppression of Unlawful Acts of Violence at Airports Serving International Civil Aviation (1988);
– Convention for the Suppression of Unlawful Acts Against the Safety of Maritime Navigation (1988);
– Protocol for the Suppression of Unlawful Acts Against the Safety of Fixed Platforms Located on the Continental Shelf (1988);
– International Convention for the Suppression of Terrorist Bombings (1997).

obviously self-incriminating (demonizing and alienating), and consequently most terrorists would not apply the label to themselves.

Terrorist tactics aim to undermine domestic economic capacity, destroy civil morale, and prompt widespread civil disobedience by assassinating public figures and/or randomly attacking the population at large in public space. Terrorist groups are (or claim to be) motivated by several different ideologies. Thus, nationalism is a frequent cause of terrorist activity (inclusive anti-colonial struggles, separatism/self-determination, irredentism); a whole spectrum of ideologies from right-wing (anti-Semitic, neo-fascist) to left-wing (Maoists, Marxist-Leninists) etc.

Although most terrorist groups, especially in Europe and Latin America, have not in fact achieved their political ends, elsewhere the situation is different. Many groups, particularly in Africa and Asia that were formerly labelled as terrorist groups, and began as opponents of colonial regimes, have legitimized themselves by forming the post-colonial government. In recent years, the Islamic State managed to control vast swathes of Iraq and Syria, with cities as large as Raqqa and Mosul.

Terrorism is characterized by the utilization of violence for political purposes and the creation of fear among the public. Thus, a terrorist can be defined as an individual involved in, or having been associated with, the commission or attempted commission of such acts (such as: sabotage by explosion or fire; killing or endangering people and/or property either by misuse of nuclear, biological, chemical materials or by conventional means and devices; hijacking of aircraft, ship or other transportation means; kidnapping or taking hostages; serious cyber- attacks) or directing, organizing, recruiting or training people for the purposes of terrorism.

Additionally, most of the national legislation considers it a serious criminal offense if a person fails to disclose information which may assist the authorities in the prevention of an act of terrorism. Other criminal offenses also prescribed by law include collecting information or possessing of information likely to be useful to foreign or domestic terrorists. This difficulty in defining terrorism has meant that it has been defined differently in different states. There is no universally recognized definition of the concept of terrorism, although many of its elements are inferred from the robust legal regime for preventing and combating terrorism.

Numerous states have adopted a solution wherein they integrate elements from international conventions into their definitions of terrorism within the framework of their legal regimes for counter-terrorism. Alternatively, some states have opted for a unified definition, often resembling that outlined in the

Terrorism Model Law[37], which identifies a terrorist as follows: 'Any individual who commits an act with the intent to cause death or serious bodily harm to a civilian, or to any other person not actively engaged in hostilities in a situation of armed conflict. This act, by its nature or context, seeks to intimidate a population or compel a Government to perform or refrain from specific actions.'

In the pursuit of this definition, certain countries have enacted laws that explicitly use the term terrorism in their titles and provide detailed descriptions of substantive offenses. These legal measures aim to ensure a clear and comprehensive understanding of terrorism within their jurisdiction, providing a solid foundation for counter-terrorism efforts and the prosecution of those involved in such acts.

Without any attempt to problematize here the 'asymmetric threats,' 'non-state actors' and 'winning the hearts and minds' theories or pre-emptive doctrines, let us state that the difference between a political party and a terrorist group is in their means – these are always criminal, on the side of terrorist groups; and legitimate, constitutionally prescribed means on the side of ordinary political parties. However, the very goal is in most of the cases identical: political influence. Political agenda is always national and aims at either ideological or territorial change on a specific, clearly defined territory and population. Since there is no international political party, it cam be argued that in fact there is also no international terrorist group. There is a sporadic transnational cooperation (coordination, exchange of operative information or tools), but the core ideas and members are always and only national. Al Qaeda represents a national identity, with members from Morocco and Yemen sharing Arab heritage. Throughout their history, Arabs predominantly lived under unified state entities, primarily the Caliphates like the Ottomans. The fragmentation into around two dozen states is a relatively new phenomenon for Arabs, one they are still adjusting to. The Islamic State, despite its self-proclaimed status as a caliphate with authority over all Muslims, functions as a terrorist organization concentrated on Iraq and Syria—ISIS, the Islamic State of Iraq and Syria. Terrorism, fundamentally, is not an ideology; rather, it often serves as a method of radical political action by a marginalized group, justified by its projected political goals.

Establishing a line of critical similarities and differences between the legitimate political party and clandestine (prescribed by law) terrorist group, we can now endorse – following the same token – the link between the

[37] United Nations, Model Law on Terrorism, sec. 2.

criminal group and corporate entity. Thus, the essential similarity between the (trans-national) organized crime group and the legitimate business enterprise is that both are profit driven – they operate to either gain, maintain or enlarge the market and profit shares. The critical difference is in the means used. On the side of organized crime grouping the means used are always (predominantly) criminal, whereas the legitimate enterprise will operate respecting the national legal framework.

However, the lasting, ultimate ambition of any parallel structure, as are organized crime (grey economic sector) or terrorist grouping (grey political sector), will be a gradual, well- orchestrated eventual legalization. It is not only the relative strength of a particular state: capability and capacity of its judiciary and effectiveness of its legal enforcement that matters. The ability of a state to achieve and maintain the social cohesion by including all segments of society to participate coherently will also be essential.

Since the existing international conventions against terrorism did not adequately address the issue of states responsibility to prevent and refrain from acts of terrorism all along, during the 1990s, the UN Security Council adopted the resolutions imposing sanctions on certain states accused of sponsoring terrorism several times. At that point it became evident that a legal instrument adopted by the UN General Assembly would provide a universally legitimate basis for combating international terrorism and avoid political controversies arising from unilateral or selective actions. To this end, a draft of a comprehensive convention against international terrorism appeared during the 53rd session of GA. Most of the parties concerned, contributed to strengthening the global consensus on combating international terrorism.

As a result of these efforts, the UNGA reaffirmed the mandate of the Ad Hoc Committee (established by Res. 51/210[38]) with its resolution 53/108[39], to elaborate a draft international convention for the Suppression of Terrorist Financing to supplement existing international instruments on terrorism.

Finally, in December 1999, the UN Convention for the Suppression of the Financing of Terrorism[40] was approved. This Convention expands the legal framework for international co-operation in the investigation, prosecution and extradition of persons engaged in (financing) terrorism. On 28 September

---

[38] United Nations Human Rights Office, *Conclusions concernant les enfants et le conflit armé au Népal*, S/AC.51/2010/4, November 11, 2010.

[39] United Nations General Assembly, Measures to Eliminate International Terrorism, A/RES/53/108 (January 26, 1999).

[40] United Nations General Assembly, International Convention for the Suppression of the Financing of Terrorism, No. 38349 (December 9, 1999).

2001, the Security Council adopted resolution 1373[41], expanding freezing obligations to persons (and certain related persons and entities) who commit or attempt to commit terrorist acts. Additionally, elaboration of the International Convention for the Suppression of Acts of Nuclear Terrorism has successfully been closed in 2005 in Vienna – further strengthening the body of universal legislations in matters related to terrorism.

The universal criminal response was developed under the auspices of the United Nations and its specialized agencies such as the International Civil Aviation Organization[42], the International Maritime Organization[43] and the International Energy Agency[44]. The international instruments cover acts of hijacking of aircraft, acts of sabotage of aircraft, acts of violence at airports, acts against the safety of maritime navigation, acts against the safety of offshore platforms located on the continental shelf. Crimes against internationally protected persons, acts of unlawful seizure and possession of nuclear materials, acts of hostage-taking, acts of detonation of terrorist explosives, acts of financing the commission of terrorist acts and nuclear terrorism committed by individuals and groups.

Finally, in 2006, the United Nations adopted Resolution 60/288[45], establishing a plan of action against terrorism, according to which member states must unequivocally condemn any act or manifestation or form of terrorism. As concrete measures to combat terrorism, the plan set out, inter alia, the obligation to prevent territories in member states from being used for the formation of terrorist groups; full cooperation in accordance with international standards; the prosecution and extradition of perpetrators; the intensification of cooperation and exchange of information aimed at preventing, coordinating and combating other crimes that are sometimes connected, such as drug or arms trafficking; checking that asylum seekers have not been involved in terrorist activities; creating regional counter-terrorism offices; the possibility of creating an international center for the fight against terrorism; implementing recommendations against money laundering;

---

[41] United Nations Security Council, Resolution 1373: Threats to International Peace and Security Caused by Terrorist Acts, S/RES/1373 (2001).

[42] International Civil Aviation Organization (ICAO), "Safe Skies, Sustainable Future," accessed September 11, 2024, https://www.icao.int/Pages/default.aspx.

[43] International Maritime Organization (IMO), "IMO Secretary-General Visits Red Sea Countries," accessed September 11, 2024, https://www.imo.org/.

[44] International Energy Agency (IEA), "Energy Technology Perspectives 2024 Out Now," accessed November 29, 2024, https://www.iea.org/.

[45] United Nations General Assembly, The United Nations Global Counter-Terrorism Strategy, A/RES/60/288 (September 20, 2006).

establishing a database of biological crimes; as well as encouraging cooperation between states and between international organizations. The United Nations Global Counter-Terrorism Strategy[46] endeavors to confront the multifaceted challenge of terrorism through four interlinked pillars. The first pillar is dedicated to addressing the conditions that foster the proliferation of terrorism. This involves efforts to identify and mitigate factors conducive to radicalization and extremism.

The second pillar focuses on establishing measures aimed at preventing and combating acts of terrorism. This includes the development and implementation of robust national and international frameworks, such as legal instruments and security protocols, to thwart terrorist activities.

The third pillar emphasizes the enhancement of states' capacities to prevent and combat terrorism. It involves initiatives to bolster the capabilities of nations in countering terrorist threats, often through capacity-building programs and technical assistance. Additionally, this pillar seeks to strengthen the role of the United Nations System in coordinating global efforts against terrorism.

Lastly, the fourth pillar centers on measures to uphold human rights for all individuals and the rule of law as the fundamental foundations in the fight against terrorism. This underscores the importance of ensuring that counter-terrorism actions are conducted within the framework of international law, with due regard for human rights standards and principles of justice.

Together, these four pillars of the United Nations Global Counter-Terrorism Strategy form a comprehensive and integrated approach to addressing the complex challenges posed by terrorism.

Within the ambit of the UN's overarching strategy to counter terrorism globally, the General Assembly, through Resolution 66/10[47], established the United Nations Counter-Terrorism Centre. This initiative is designed to provide backing to member states, international and regional organizations, civil society groups, and other entities engaged in counter-terrorism efforts as they implement the Global Counter-Terrorism Strategy Similarly, in alignment with this approach, the General Assembly further solidified support

---

[46] United Nations, "UN Global Counter-Terrorism Strategy," accessed December 12, 2024, https://www.un.org/counterterrorism/un-global-counter-terrorism-strategy.

[47] United Nations General Assembly, Resolution 66/10: United Nations Counter-Terrorism Centre, A/RES/66/10 (December 7, 2011).

to member states with Resolution 71/291 of June 2017[48] by establishing the UN Global Counter Terrorism Coordination Compact.

Other relevant actors in the fights against terrorism, are the WCO (World Customs Organization[49]), Interpol, and the IAEA (International Atomic Energy Agency[50]), which conducts a detection and response training programs for custom and other officials (programs mostly emphasized on the prevention of nuclear smuggling).

Moreover, the International Atomic Energy Agency assists CEE/SEE, Central–East Asian and Pacific countries in establishing their domestic legal frameworks to comply with the international. standards, including the national laws governing the safe and peaceful usage of nuclear energy (nuclear legislation & regulations, including non-proliferation and physical protection of nuclear material and facilities).

The International Civil Aviation Organization[51] (ICAO) effectively provides financial, technical, and material support to states in enhancing aviation security measures. This assistance encompasses initiatives aimed at bolstering security measures for both aircraft and airports serving international civil aviation

IMO (International Maritime Organization[52]) organizes specially designed training programs to combat crimes connected with international terrorism (safety of maritime navigation, safety of fixed platforms, open-seas piracy, etc.).

TPB of CICP/ODCCP (Terrorism Prevention Branch, special division, created in 1999) is a clearing-house for matters related to international terrorism[53]. It is very active in research (e.g., the questionnaires regularly sent to each of the Institutes of UN criminal justice network). In relation to legal assistance, TPB has a well-established cooperation and permanent consultations with the Sixth Committee of the United Nations General Assembly and UN Office of Legal Affairs in New York (particularly with a

---

[48] United Nations General Assembly, Resolution 71/291: Strengthening the Capability of the United Nations System to Assist Member States in Implementing the UN Global Counter-Terrorism Strategy, A/RES/71/291 (June 15, 2017).

[49] World Customs Organization, accessed November 24, 2024, https://www.wcoomd.org/.

[50] International Atomic Energy Agency (IAEA), accessed November 24, 2024, https://www.iaea.org/.

[51] International Civil Aviation Organization (ICAO), *Convention on International Civil Aviation* ("Chicago Convention"), 15 U.N.T.S. 295 (December 7, 1944).

[52] United Nations, Convention on the International Maritime Organization, adopted March 6, 1948, entered into force March 17, 1958.

[53] United Nations, "Terrorism Prevention Branch," accessed September 30, 2024, https://www.unodc.org/unodc/en/terrorism/aboutus.html.

Codification Division of the Legal Affairs Office, which gathers data on national laws and regulations regarding the prevention and suppression of international terrorism).

UNDCP, Europol, UNESCO[54], OIC[55], OAU[56], SAARC, EU/EC, Council of Europe and other affiliated or non-affiliated bodies, agencies and regional organizations are, also, taking their measures to prevent; detect; collect, disseminate, and exchange information on; suppress; punish and eliminate international terrorism.

Example (of non-affiliated entity) includes the Naïf Arab Academy for Security Sciences[57] in Riyadh, which annually offers dozens of comprehensive training courses on combating terrorism for the Arab JHA community.

In contrast to other criminal activities like human trafficking, drug trafficking, and corruption, there is no universal standard that addresses terrorism in a broad, generic manner. However, there exist multiple complementary conventions that specifically target various aspects of terrorism, as listed below.

Global International Instruments:

- 1963 Convention on Offenses and Certain Other Acts Committed on Board Aircraft[58] (Tokyo Convention).

This Convention outlines jurisdictional issues, the powers of aircraft commanders, and provisions against the unlawful seizure of aircraft.

- 1970 Convention for the Suppression of Unlawful Seizure of Aircraft[59] (Hague Convention).

This Convention focuses on the criminalization of aircraft hijackings.

---

[54] United Nations Educational, Scientific and Cultural Organization (UNESCO), *UNESCO Universal Declaration on Cultural Diversity* (November 2, 2001).

[55] Organization of Islamic Cooperation (OIC), "The Collective Voice of the Muslim World," accessed September 11, 2024, https://www.oic-oci.org/.

[56] Organization of African Unity (OAU), Convention on the Prevention and Combating of Terrorism, June 14, 1999.

[57] Naif Arab University for Security Sciences (NAUSS), "NAUSS Signs a Memorandum of Understanding with the United Nations Counter-Terrorism Center (UNCCT)," accessed November 24, 2024, https://nauss.edu.sa/en-us/news/Pages/2-10-2021.aspx.

[58] ICAO, Convention on Offenses and Certain Acts Committed on Board Aircraft, September 14, 1963.

[59] United Nations, Convention for the Suppression of Unlawful Seizure of Aircraft, UN Treaty Series, December 16, 1970.

- 1971 Convention for the Suppression of Unlawful Acts against the Safety of Civil Aviation[60] (Montreal Convention).

Targeting acts of aviation sabotage, such as bombings aboard aircraft.

- 1973 Convention on the Prevention and Punishment of Crimes against Internationally Protected Persons, including Diplomatic Agents[61] (UN Convention).

This Convention aims to protect senior governmental officials and diplomats.

- 1979 International Convention against the Taking of Hostages[62] (UN Convention)

Designed to combat the taking of hostages as a form of terrorism.

- 1980 Convention on the Physical Protection of Nuclear Material[63] (UN Convention)

Concerned with preventing the unlawful taking and use of nuclear materials.

- 1988 Protocol for the Suppression of Unlawful Acts of Violence at Airports Serving International Civil Aviation[64] (Montreal Protocol).

This Protocol extends and supplements the Montreal Convention of 1971, focusing on enhancing air safety.

- 1988 UN Convention for the Suppression of Unlawful Acts against the Safety of Maritime Navigation[65] (Rome Convention).

It targets terrorist activities on ships, enhancing maritime security.

---

[60] ICAO, Convention for the Suppression of Unlawful Acts Against the Safety of Civil Aviation, 974 U.N.T.S. 177 (September 23, 1971).

[61] United Nations General Assembly, Convention on the Prevention and Punishment of Crimes Against Internationally Protected Persons, Including Diplomatic Agents, A/RES/3166 (December 14, 1973).

[62] United Nations General Assembly, International Convention Against the Taking of Hostages, No. 21931 (November 17, 1979).

[63] United Nations General Assembly, *Convention on the Physical Protection of Nuclear Material*, No. 24631 (October 26, 1979).

[64] United Nations, Protocol for the Suppression of Unlawful Acts of Violence at Airports Serving International Civil Aviation, supplementary to the Convention for the Suppression of Unlawful Acts Against the Safety of Civil Aviation, UN Treaty Series (February 24, 1988).

[65] United Nations General Assembly, Convention for the Suppression of Unlawful Acts Against the Safety of Maritime Navigation, No. 29004 (March 10, 1988).

- 1988 Protocol for the Suppression of Unlawful Acts against the Safety of Fixed Platforms Located on the Continental Shelf[66] (Rome Protocol).

It addresses terrorist attacks on fixed offshore platforms.

- 1991 Convention on the Marking of Plastic Explosives for the Purpose of Detection[67] (Montreal Convention).

This Convention involves the chemical marking of plastic explosives for international identification to combat aircraft sabotage.

- 1997 International Convention for the Suppression of Terrorist Bombings[68] (UN Convention).

It expands the legal framework for international cooperation in investigating, prosecuting, and extraditing persons involved in terrorist bombings.

- 1999 International Convention for the Suppression of the Financing of Terrorism[69] (UN Convention).

This Convention aims to enhance international cooperation in investigating, prosecuting, and extraditing individuals involved in financing terrorism.

- Security Council Resolution 1373 on International Cooperation to Combat Threats of Terrorism[70] (2001).

This Resolution emphasizes international cooperation among member states to combat threats to international peace and security posed by terrorist attacks.

---

[66]United Nations General Assembly, Protocol for the Suppression of Unlawful Acts Against the Safety of Fixed Platforms Located on the Continental Shelf, UNTS 1678, I-29004 (March 10, 1988).

[67] United Nations General Assembly, Convention on the Marking of Plastic Explosives for the Purpose of Detection (March 1, 1991).

[68]United Nations General Assembly, International Convention for the Suppression of Terrorist Bombings, No. 37517 (December 15, 1997).

[69] United Nations General Assembly, International Convention for the Suppression of the Financing of Terrorism, No. 38349 (December 9, 1999).

[70] United Nations Security Council, Security Council Resolution 1373 (2001): Threats to International Peace and Security Caused by Terrorist Acts, S/RES/1373 (September 28, 2001).

- 2005 International Convention for the Suppression of Acts of Nuclear Terrorism[71] (UN Convention).

It criminalizes acts of nuclear terrorism and enhances international cooperation in preventing, investigating, prosecuting, and extraditing individuals engaged in such acts.

There has also been considerable progress at the regional level These regional conventions and protocols highlight the diverse approaches taken by various regional organizations to address the complex challenges posed by terrorism within their respective regions. They underscore the importance of international cooperation, legal frameworks, and joint efforts in combating the threat of terrorism across borders.

- 1971 OAS Convention to Prevent and Punish Terrorism Acts of International Significance[72] (Organization of American States Convention).

This Convention, adopted by the Organization of American States (OAS), expands upon the scope of the General Assembly Resolution on Acts of Terrorism. It particularly focuses on crimes such as the kidnapping of persons and related extortion, providing a legal framework for addressing such acts within the OAS region.

- 1977 European Convention on the Suppression of Terrorism[73] (Council of Europe Convention).

Signed by all European Union (EU) member states by 1979, this Convention serves as a foundational element for the EU's Maastricht Treaty of 1992. It aims to strengthen cooperation in the areas of justice and home affairs concerning the suppression of terrorism.

- 1987 SAARC Regional Convention on Suppression of Terrorism[74] (South Asian Association for Regional Cooperation Convention).

---

[71] United Nations General Assembly, International Convention for the Suppression of Acts of Nuclear Terrorism, A/RES/59/290 (April 15, 2005).

[72] Organization of American States (OAS), Convention to Prevent and Punish the Acts of Terrorism Taking the Form of Crimes Against Persons and Related Extortion That Are of International Significance, OAS Treaty Series, No. 37 (February 2, 1971).

[73] Council of Europe, European Convention on the Suppression of Terrorism, ETS No. 90 (January 27, 1977).

[74] South Asian Association for Regional Cooperation (SAARC), Regional Convention on the Suppression of Terrorism (November 4, 1987).

Created for the member states of the South Asian Association for Regional Cooperation (SAARC), namely Bangladesh, Bhutan, India, Maldives, Nepal, Pakistan, and Sri Lanka, this Convention underscores the principles laid out in UN Resolution 2625[75] (XXV). It highlights the need for collective action against terrorist activities, building upon agreements from the 1985 Dhaka SAARC Summit.

- 2004 Additional Protocol to the SAARC Convention[76] (SAARC Additional Protocol).

This Protocol supplements the original SAARC Convention, providing a framework for regional mechanisms of implementation and information exchange related to terrorist acts.

- 1998 Arab Convention on the Suppression of Terrorism[77] (League of Arab States Convention).

This Convention, adopted by the League of Arab States, aims to enhance international cooperation in the investigation, prosecution, and extradition of individuals engaged in terrorist activities within the Arab region.

- 1999 OAU/AU Convention on the Prevention and Combat of Terrorism[78] (Organization of African Unity/African Union Convention).

Adopted by the Organization of African Unity[79] (OAU), later the African Union[80] (AU), this Convention establishes a legal framework for preventing and combating terrorism within the African region. It emphasizes international cooperation in investigating, prosecuting, and extraditing individuals involved in such activities.

---

[75] United Nations General Assembly, Declaration on Principles of International Law Concerning Friendly Relations and Cooperation Among States in Accordance with the Charter of the United Nations, A/RES/2625(XXV) (October 24, 1970).

[76] SAARC, Additional Protocol to the SAARC Regional Convention on Suppression of Terrorism (January 6, 2004).

[77] League of Arab States, Arab Convention on the Suppression of Terrorism (April 22, 1998).

[78] Organization of African Unity (OAU), OAU Convention on the Prevention and Combating of Terrorism (June 14, 1999).

[79] Organization of African Unity (OAU), Charter of the Organization of African Unity (May 25, 1963).

[80] Heads of State and Government of the Member States of the Organization of African Unity, Constitutive Act of the African Union, OAU (July 1, 2000).

- 2004 Protocol to the OAU Convention on the Prevention and Combating of Terrorism[81] (African Union Protocol).

This Protocol builds upon the OAU/AU Convention, providing mechanisms for regional implementation, prevention, and combating of terrorist acts.

- 1999 OIC Convention on Combating International Terrorism[82] (Organization of Islamic Conference Convention).

Adopted by the Organization of Islamic Conference (OIC) member states, this Convention focuses on enhancing international cooperation in investigating, prosecuting, and extraditing individuals engaged in terrorism within the OIC region.

- 2002 Inter-American Convention Against Terrorism[83] (Organization of American States Convention).

This Convention, signed by countries within the Organization of American States (OAS), establishes a legal framework for preventing, combating, and cooperating on terrorism-related issues. It emphasizes joint efforts in investigating, prosecuting, and extraditing individuals involved in terrorist activities within the Americas.

- 2005 Council of Europe Convention on the Prevention of Terrorism (Council of Europe Convention). United Nations General Assembly, *International Convention for the Suppression of the Financing of Terrorism*, No. 38349 (December 9, 1999).

Signed by European countries, this Convention aims to prevent terrorism through cooperation, particularly focusing on areas such as state jurisdiction, investigation, and mutual legal assistance. It seeks to enhance international collaboration in addressing the threat of terrorism.

---

[81] African Union, Protocol to the OAU Convention on the Prevention and Combating of Terrorism (July 8, 2004).

[82] Organization of Islamic Cooperation (OIC), Convention of the Organization of the Islamic Conference on Combating International Terrorism, Annex to Resolution No. 59/26-P (July 1, 1999).

[83] Organization of American States (OAS), Inter-American Convention Against Terrorism (March 6, 2002).

- 2005 Council of Europe Convention on Laundering, Search, Seizure and Confiscation of the Proceeds from Crime and on the Financing of Terrorism (Council of Europe Convention).

This Convention represents the first international treaty covering both the prevention and control of money laundering and the financing of terrorism. It aims to combat the financial aspects of terrorism, facilitating the tracing and confiscation of illicit funds.

- 2007 ASEAN Convention on Counter Terrorism (ASEAN Convention).

Adopted by the Association of Southeast Asian Nations (ASEAN), this Convention focuses on terrorist offenses, cooperative measures, and political exceptions within the ASEAN region. It includes provisions for mutual legal assistance and the designation of central authorities for effective coordination in counter-terrorism efforts.

- 2017 Additional Protocol to the Council of Europe Convention on the Prevention of Terrorism[84] (Council of Europe Convention).

This Protocol criminalizes specific acts related to terrorism, such as participating in terrorist associations or groups, receiving terrorist training, traveling abroad for terrorism, and financing or organizing travel for terrorist purposes. It serves as an extension of the Council of Europe Convention's framework for preventing terrorism.

The global effort to counter terrorism needs a holistic response. Despite the absence of a universally accepted definition of terrorism, legal frameworks exist to delineate specific acts as constituting terrorism. Usually focused on specific local goals, it leverages international networks like organized crime groups, relying on illegal activities like human trafficking and drug trafficking for financial support. This underscores the necessity of combating terrorism through the lens of the UNTOC and fostering extensive collaboration among nations. The body of international agreements, complemented by UN resolutions and national legislation, establishes a solid legal infrastructure that facilitates effective cooperation between states. The central role of the UN is evident in its formulation of legal frameworks and strategic initiatives to combat terrorism. However, in the same way as for other transnational crimes,

---

[84] Council of Europe, Additional Protocol to the Council of Europe Convention on the Prevention of Terrorism (May 19, 2015).

new challenges arise due to the forces of globalization, technological advances, the complexity of tracking illicit financial flows and the intricate interplay between terrorist groups and other criminal organizations.

The nature of terrorism evolves, often acting as transnational criminal organizations. Therefore, the response to this evolving threat requires adaptation, employing specific counter-terrorism legislation alongside instruments aimed at combating transnational crime. A comprehensive and contemporary approach is imperative to effectively address emerging manifestations of terrorism. It is a global threat, but localized in its targets. However, the response must be unfailingly global, addressing any space of impunity where terrorists nurture and grow. Therefore, the role of the United Nations is unique in this area, with all states being obliged by the international community to confront terrorism in all its forms.

4.3. Drug Trafficking

The global battle against drug trafficking stands out as one of the most enduring and challenging struggles of the 20th and 21st centuries. Undoubtedly, drug trafficking represents the most profitable criminal enterprise, requiring states worldwide to devote enormous resources to its containment. Its impact extends far beyond monetary gains, serving as a destabilizing force within societies, fueling severe public health crises, and resulting in thousands of fatalities globally. Moreover, its commercialization often serves as a gateway to the proliferation of criminal activities.

The power of drug trafficking organizations is evident in their ability to challenge and even contest the authority of states. These criminal groups create spheres of impunity, thrive in societies marked by limited opportunities, and push vulnerable young people into the dangerous world of drug trafficking.

Persistent problems in the fight against drug gangs, coupled with the failure to eradicate drug trafficking despite major efforts, have led to debates about drug legalization or decriminalization. However, this discourse, though appealing to some, often diverges from the historical context and the original motivations behind the global fight against drug trafficking.

The origins of the global fight against drug trafficking can be situated before the well-known US-led fight against drug trafficking in Latin American countries. Its roots trace back to the epidemic that ravaged China, reaching a catastrophic scale with an estimated 10 million opium addicts - representing a quarter of the adult male population. This crisis led to the landmark 1912 International Opium Convention[85], marking the inception of the first international treaty against drug trafficking. Subsequently, the League of Nations took up the cause in 1920, making it a central focus of its mission[86].

The drug war has achieved significant progress in containment and reduction. Early international efforts have helped curb the destructive impact of drug trafficking on societies worldwide.[87]

While a comprehensive approach (including demand reduction) is necessary, it would be unfair to claim that the fight against drug trafficking has been ineffective. The United States' battle against drug trafficking began in the 1970s with the government's declaration of the "war on drugs," primarily in response to the rising influx of drugs, especially from Colombia. At the same time, Colombia was embroiled in its own struggle, where the state faced off against powerful drug cartels, often finding itself overwhelmed by their economic and political influence.

The illicit drug trade is so economically powerful that its intricate networks can destabilize entire states. When law enforcement and international pressure intensify in one region, these criminal networks have an incredible ability to adapt, often shifting their operations to new territories. A prime example of this evolution is how, over time, a significant portion of the drug trafficking directed toward the United States shifted into the hands of Mexican cartels. This shift demonstrates how trafficking routes themselves can evolve in response to changing circumstances.

In recent years, a new drug trafficking corridor has emerged from South America, using the West African route. This shift further illustrates the constantly changing dynamics of the global drug trade and the ongoing challenge faced by law enforcement agencies worldwide[88].

Cartels have taken advantage of instability in West Africa, using the region as a gateway to Western countries - demonstrating just how adaptable these criminal networks can be. Their flexibility is also seen in the way they

---

[85] United Nations General Assembly, International Opium Convention (The Hague, January 23, 1912).

[86] League of Nations, Agreement Concerning the Suppression of the Manufacture of, Internal Trade in, and Use of, Prepared Opium (Geneva, February 11, 1925); and Protocol Amending the Agreements, Conventions, and Protocols on Narcotic Drugs, concluded at The Hague (1912), Geneva (1925, 1931).

[87] United Nations Office on Drugs and Crime, *A Century of International Drug Control* (Vienna: UNODC, 2008), 7–10.

[88] United Nations Office on Drugs and Crime, *Drug Trafficking as a Security Threat in West Africa* (2008), 7. Accessed November 24, 2024. https://www.unodc.org/documents/data-and-analysis/Studies/Drug-Trafficking-WestAfrica-English.pdf.

restructure operations, especially in major markets across Asia and the Pacific[89].

The violence, destruction, and loss of life caused by drug trafficking affect not only countries of origin, but also transit and destination countries. Transit countries are also exposed to considerable risks and vulnerabilities[90].

Moreover, the challenges posed by globalization present an additional layer of complexity in combating drug trafficking. The exponential growth of world trade renders the control of goods an immensely challenging task. Consequently, any effective response to drug trafficking necessitates a globally coordinated effort. The pressure exerted by the international community to prevent certain regions from becoming havens of immunity is fundamental to this endeavor.

The legal instruments aimed at combating the complex challenges posed by transnational organized crime associated with narcotics trace their roots back to the early 20th century[91]:

In the midst of post-World War II reforms, the Convention on Narcotic Drugs was adopted at the international level in 1961[92]. This landmark treaty was intended to replace previous agreements and establish a unified framework for international drug control.

On this basis, the 1971 Convention on Psychotropic Substances[93] as well as the 1988 Convention against Illicit Trafficking in Narcotic Drugs[94] were subsequently adopted, both of which further expanded the global framework for combating drug-related crime.

The 1961 Convention on Narcotic Drugs plays a crucial role in the joint fight against illicit drug trafficking. It establishes a comprehensive framework for cooperation and law enforcement between nations. It provides relevant definitions for fundamental terms such as "cannabis," and "coca bush." It outlines procedures and measures aimed at controlling substances listed in the

---

89 Anthea McCarthy-Jones, Caroline Doyle, and Mark Turner, "From Hierarchies to Networks: The Organizational Evolution of the International Drug Trade," *International Journal of Law, Crime and Justice* (August 2020).

90 United Nations Office of Drugs and Crime, *Drug Trafficking as a Security Threat in West Africa*.

91 United Nations, *UN Treaty Collection*, accessed September 27, 2024, https://treaties.un.org/Pages/CTCTreaties.aspx?id=6&subid=A.

92 United Nations General Assembly, 1972 Protocol Amending the Single Convention on Narcotic Drugs, 1961, A/RES/3444 (December 9, 1972).

93 United Nations General Assembly, 1971 Convention on Psychotropic Substances, A/RES/3443 (December 9, 1975).

94 United Nations, United Nations Convention Against Illicit Traffic in Narcotic Drugs and Psychotropic Substances (December 19, 1988).

Convention and recognizes the intricate web of drug trafficking that extends across borders, and underscores the imperative for concerted action and cooperation among nations. It emphasizes the shared responsibility of member states to enact legislative and administrative measures within their respective jurisdictions to effectively counter the transnational movement of narcotics.

The 1961 Convention also emphasizes the fundamental role of international control bodies, such as the Commission on Narcotic Drugs and the International Narcotics Control Board. These control mechanisms play a crucial role in monitoring the implementation of the provisions of the Convention, coordinating global efforts, and preventing the illicit drug trade from strengthening transnational organized crime networks.

In addition, the 1961 Convention underscores the significance of clear reporting mechanisms and robust accountability measures. It stresses the need for transparency in estimating drug requirements, providing comprehensive statistical data, and sharing pertinent information on drug-related activities among member states. These measures are instrumental in ensuring compliance with the Convention's objectives and preventing the diversion of controlled substances into illicit markets.

Afterwards, the 1971 Convention on Psychotropic Substances laid down a systematic and detailed framework for the evaluation and control of substances, particularly addressing the global challenges posed by the illicit drug trade. It establishes a structured process that allows for the addition, transfer, or deletion of substances within the Convention's schedules.

It also foresees the exchange of information regarding substances that are not yet under international control or require adjustments within the schedules. When a State party or the World Health Organization[95] (hereinafter, WHO) identifies such substances, they must notify the Secretary-General, who then disseminates this information to relevant stakeholders. This exchange is crucial for well-informed decision-making and fostering collaboration among member states.

The WHO plays a fundamental role in this process by conducting assessments on substances, particularly focusing on their potential for dependence, central nervous system effects, and abuse. Factors such as medical utility, abuse potential, and public health impact are carefully weighed during this evaluation. The goal is to establish the most appropriate level of control for each substance, based on the identified risks and benefits.

---

[95] United Nations General Assembly, Entry into Force of the Constitution of the World Health Organization, A/RES/131 (November 17, 1948).

Additionally, the 1971 Convention outlines specific provisions such as the prohibition of import, special provisions for international transport of substances for first-aid purposes, requirements for inspections, and reporting obligations. These measures collectively aim to enhance cooperation among states parties, promote regulatory compliance, and combat the illicit drug trade and abuse of psychotropic substances on a global scale.

However, it was not until 1988 that a Convention explicitly designed for the transnational fight against organized crime was introduced. The United Nations Convention against Illicit Traffic in Narcotic Drugs and Psychotropic Substances entered into force in 1988. The entry into force of this Convention marked the culmination of the legal framework for the global control, prevention, and fight against drug trafficking, which is still in force today. This evolution took place in parallel with the important complementary role played by the UNTOC.

The 1988 Convention against Illicit Traffic in Narcotic Drugs and Psychotropic Substances represents a key international instrument aimed at addressing the multifaceted challenges posed by the illicit drug trade within the context of transnational organized crime. It establishes the commitment of the states parties to oversee not only the substances explicitly covered by the Convention but also those materials commonly utilized in the illicit manufacturing of drugs. This expanded supervision seeks to disrupt the supply chain of illegal narcotics, thereby curtailing the operations of transnational criminal networks engaged in drug trafficking.

The 1988 Convention underscores the obligation of member states to enact legislative measures within their territories to rigorously enforce its provisions. Emphasizing cooperation among states, this commitment promotes strict control over all aspects of drug-related activities, spanning from production to distribution, thereby fostering a collaborative approach in combating transnational organized crime associated with narcotics.

The states commit to providing each other with comprehensive assistance in investigations, prosecutions, and judicial proceedings related to drug offenses. This includes sharing evidence, executing searches, and providing necessary information, thereby fostering effective cross-border cooperation in combating transnational organized crime associated with narcotics.

Measures are outlined to prevent the trade of materials and equipment used in illicit drug production and efforts to eradicate the cultivation of illicit plants while respecting human rights and environmental concerns, thereby addressing the root causes of drug-related crimes.

Moreover, the 1988 Convention allows for controlled delivery of illicit consignments and commits parties to monitoring the manufacture, distribution, and trade of substances frequently used in illicit manufacturing, ensuring proper labelling and documentation, thereby enhancing international law enforcement efforts.

Additionally, the Convention provides parties with the flexibility to adopt stricter measures if necessary, to combat drug trafficking effectively, while respecting existing rights and obligations under earlier drug control treaties, thereby ensuring a comprehensive and adaptable framework to address the evolving challenges posed by transnational organized crime in the realm of narcotics.

The Convention on Psychotropic Substances is an essential tool for international cooperation, legal assistance, and law enforcement strategies to combat illicit drug trafficking in the context of transnational organized crime. By fostering collaboration between nations and establishing clear guidelines for action.

However, it is evident that combatting drug trafficking necessitates a comprehensive approach, extending beyond mere prevention and law enforcement responses. The fight against drug trafficking is both urgent and crucial, given its significant impact on public health and the security and stability of countries. While penalties, police efforts, and criminal law enforcement can help mitigate trafficking and its escalation, they have, thus far, proven inadequate for its eradication. Hence, nations must intensify international cooperation, utilize the tools provided by UNTOC, and pursue policies aimed at reducing demand, which lies at the core of drug trafficking.

However, the battle against drug trafficking cannot be seen as a lost cause. It is crucial to prevent impunity for the organizations involved. These groups often destabilize and create environments ripe for various forms of crime, capitalizing on the lack of opportunities for youth and even fostering a misguided glorification of drug trafficking entities. Despite its complexities, the global effort against drug trafficking has proven effective in at least containing and deterring trafficking activities. However, amidst the current global turbulence, characterized by potential reduced international cooperation, we must continue to stress the importance of this fight. It is crucial to maintain and promote judicial and police collaboration, even in the difficult times we are facing, which can be used by criminal organizations to expand their power.

Chapter 5

New Era, New Challenges

5.1. Cybercrime

The digital environment mirrors many of the challenges present in the physical world. Just as our environment struggles with pollution, cyberspace faces its own form of contamination.

In this digital environment, information plays a central role: the content, context, means, and end. The digital world tries to turn information into something like currency, much like how oil is valuable to national economies. In this context, personal data is like gold - it powers and drives the digital system.

Unsurprisingly, cyberspace is getting rougher as it becomes more about making money and using it as a weapon. This hostility is particularly evident in the invasion of privacy, with escalating incidents of personal information being exposed without adequate protection. How can we protect people and their rights in this changing digital world?

While the Internet has expanded our access to information and opportunities, it has also facilitated criminal activities. Cyberbullying, online fraud, child pornography, spying, and cyberattacks are just some of the crimes committed online. These digital platforms are also used for other crimes, such as terrorism or human trafficking, where criminals use the Internet to find victims.

Cybercrimes often go unpunished due to the substantial challenges involved in their investigation. Effective collaboration between private entities and state authorities is essential, requiring a delicate balance between safeguarding user privacy and combating criminal activities. Striking this balance is paramount, as it determines how much users' privacy is guaranteed while fulfilling the obligation to prevent and prosecute cybercrimes. Consequently, the escalation of cybercrime underscores the pressing need for a global and decisive response. Since internet crimes frequently pose grave threats to individuals, property, and the stability of states, addressing this issue has become increasingly urgent.

The Internet primarily serves as a powerful tool for criminal organizations to perpetrate a range of crimes, many of which are traditional offenses occurring on both national and international scales.

Classic internet frauds illustrate this trend, utilizing the Internet's anonymity to facilitate identity theft and phishing schemes. These scams proliferate globally, orchestrated by criminal syndicates operating across different regions with impunity, protected from investigation due to insufficient international cooperation.

However, beyond these prevailing frauds, there are crimes that urgently demand our attention as they pose significant threats to individual and state security. One such threat is cyberterrorism, a term coined in 1980[1]. This phenomenon, which sees terrorists using computers and the Internet for their nefarious activities, is a clear and present danger. It transcends borders, making a transnational approach crucial for effective combat.

The Internet serves as an indispensable tool for terrorist networks[2], facilitating activities such as programming, psychological warfare, fundraising, radicalization, and training. For instance, Al-Qaeda utilized online platforms to coordinate and disseminate information during the September 11 attacks, highlighting the pivotal role of the Internet in modern-day terrorism.

Criminal networks engage in various transnational crimes using the Internet, like drug trafficking, arms trafficking, counterfeit medicines[3], and money laundering. Moreover, they exploit the digital landscape for other illicit activities, such as extortion through illegally obtained information and computer piracy.

Human trafficking is significantly affected by these digital advancements. Social networks serve as crucial recruitment grounds, making it imperative for companies to implement effective systems for detecting trafficking in human beings. Alarmingly, a large percentage of children and adolescents are active on the Internet, making them vulnerable targets for traffickers who exploit false identities to lure victims into meetings.

---

1 Nadiah Khaeriah Kadir, Judhariksawan, and Maskun, "Terrorism and Cyberspace: A Phenomenon of Cyber-Terrorism as Transnational Crimes," *Fiat Justisia* 13, no. 4 (2020): 335.

2 J. F. Binder and J. Kenyon, "Terrorism and the Internet: How Dangerous Is Online Radicalization?" *Frontiers in Psychology* 13 (October 13, 2022): 997390. https://doi.org/10.3389/fpsyg.2022.997390.

3 Oscar Alarcón Jiménez et al., *Construyendo los Derechos Humanos en Estrasburgo: el Tribunal Europeo de Derechos Humanos y el Consejo de Europa* (Valencia: Tirant Lo Blanch, 2020), 483.

The Internet is a common tool for carrying out human trafficking crimes, with pornography networks being a paradigmatic example. Without stringent checks to ensure consent, these networks may unwittingly propagate exploitation. Therefore, internet-based companies need to remain vigilant for signs of trafficking in human beings. Otherwise, there should be regulations, as required by the Palermo Protocol, which make them liable for the crime of trafficking in human beings for failing to take the necessary compliance measures.

Combating cybercrime poses significant challenges, particularly due to its cross-border nature; existing global laws are often inadequate, allowing criminals to evade justice. Addressing these shortcomings requires a concerted effort to strengthen international cooperation[4].

On 24 December 2024, the United Nations General Assembly (UNGA) adopted the UN Convention against Cybercrime, marking a significant milestone in the global fight against cybercrime[5], aimed at creating a comprehensive international framework to tackle this pressing issue. With the growing prevalence of cyber threats that exploit personal data, disrupt national security, and undermine economic stability, this Convention seeks to enhance international cooperation among member states. Key aspects include clear definitions of various forms of cybercrime, established procedures for mutual legal assistance, and measures for technical assistance and capacity building. The Convention emphasizes the need for a coordinated global response to effectively combat cybercrime and its areas of impunity, providing a structured approach to prevent and prosecute offenses that transcend national borders and threaten individual rights.

The United Nations Cybercrime Convention establishes a comprehensive framework for combating cybercrime, emphasizing jurisdictional cooperation, evidence gathering, and the protection of human rights. It requires states to claim jurisdiction over offenses committed on their territory, fosters collaboration on investigations, and promotes technical assistance, particularly for developing countries. However, the Convention has faced significant criticism from human rights organizations and privacy advocates. Concerns center on the potential misuse of its provisions by authoritarian regimes, leading to increased surveillance and censorship. Critics argue for

---

[4] A. Bajrektarevic and D. Karantzeni, *Cybersecurity: Essentials – Institutions, Instruments, Types and Forms* (New York: NOVA Science Publishers, 2015).

[5] *United Nations, United Nations Convention Against Cybercrime: Strengthening International Cooperation for Combating Certain Crimes Committed by Means of Information and Communications Technology Systems*, Hanoi, December 24, 2024.

clearer safeguards to protect against intrusive surveillance and to ensure transparency, asserting that the Convention's broad legal language could undermine fundamental rights like privacy and freedom of expression. Additionally, its cross-border data-sharing provisions raise issues of jurisdictional overreach, posing risks to due process and potentially hindering legitimate cybersecurity research.

Besides the United Nations Convention, the main instrument has been the Council of Europe Convention against Cybercrime, which was the first international instrument against cybercrime. As the first legally binding treaty specifically targeting cybercrime, it included the criminalization of cyber offenses, and established fundamental rules for international cooperation. For its part, Interpol has prioritized combating cybercrime among its main objectives. UN resolutions such as the Delhi Declaration[6] on countering the use of new and emerging technologies for terrorist purposes underscore the global recognition of the issue. At a worldwide level, initiatives like the Cybercrime Atlas launched by the World Economic Forum's Partnership Against Cybercrime[7] in January 2023 illustrate concerted attempts to map and understand the cybercriminal landscape. Non-governmental organizations such as the Anti-Phishing Working Group[8], the European NGO Alliance for Child Safety Online[9], the International Association of Internet Hotlines[10], the Internet Watch Foundation[11], and the RAND Corporation[12] play pivotal roles in combating various facets of cybercrime through research, advocacy, and collaboration with law enforcement agencies. Additionally, Interpol's mandate to facilitate international cooperation among law enforcement agencies underscores the recognition of cybercrime's transnational nature and the imperative for coordinated responses on a global scale.

---

[6] United Nations Security Council Counter-Terrorism Committee, *Delhi Declaration on Countering the Use of New and Emerging Technologies for Terrorist Purposes*, New Delhi, October 29, 2022.

[7] Cybercrime Atlas, "Building a Shared Knowledge Base to Disrupt Cybercrime," accessed November 30, 2024, https://initiatives.weforum.org/cybercrime-atlas/home.

[8] World Economic Forum, "Our Mission," accessed November 24, 2024, https://www.weforum.org/.

[9] ENACSO, *European NGO Alliance for Child Safety Online*, accessed September 11, 2024, http://www.enacso.eu/.

[10] INHOPE, "Somos una red mundial de 54 líneas de emergencia," accessed September 25, 2024, https://www.inhope.org/EN.

[11] Internet Watch Foundation, "Report Online Child Sexual Abuse," accessed November 11, 2024, https://www.iwf.org.uk/.

[12] RAND Corporation, "About RAND," accessed November 14, 2024, https://www.rand.org/about.html.

The approval of the Convention against cybercrime is a milestone in the fight against cybercrime. However, the rapid development of AI brings significant opportunities and undeniable risks, as malicious actors increasingly exploit these technologies for criminal purposes.

5.2. Artificial Intelligence

Artificial intelligence presents an unprecedented challenge, with the potential to profoundly transform our lives - for better or worse. It is currently being used by criminal networks, actively reshaping the landscape of transnational cybercrime. Yet the implications of AI extend far beyond the legal sphere, reaching into the existential and philosophical dimensions, challenging us to reconsider the essence of humanity itself.

To grasp the magnitude of this phenomenon, a multidimensional analysis is required—one that encompasses not only legal and ethical considerations but also the deeper existential questions that AI inevitably provokes.

Only through a comprehensive approach can we hope to devise effective strategies to confront the multifarious challenges posed by artificial intelligence.

Throughout the vast expanse of human history, progress and its dissemination have been a slow, sporadic, and often laborious process. Even during the illustrious era of Alexander, the Great, and the renowned Library of Alexandria, our knowledge transfers, though steady, were still analogue and conservative, our development occurred at a notably slow pace. However, with the advent of AI, this historical pattern has been disrupted, marking a significant departure in our civilization's trajectory.

When our sporadic breakthroughs finally became faster than their infrequent transmissions, that marked a point of our departure. Our civilizations started significantly differentiating themselves in their techno-agrarian, politico-military, ethno-religious or ideological, and economic setups. Soon, the Grand Discoveries (Europe's shift to the West) transformed wars and famine from low-impact and local ones into more extensive and cross-continental ones.

In Europe, technological breakthroughs, patents, and discoveries accelerated, reconfiguring societies in ways not seen elsewhere. It ultimately marked the birth of several European empires, their (liberal) schools (and consequent imperial weaponization of knowledge).

For the past few centuries, we have lived in fear but dreamt of hope – all for the sake of modern times. From WWI to www, humanity has seen tremendous breakthroughs. But do these advances truly lead us toward greater fairness, harmony, and reconciliation?

Thus, has our world ever been more than an idea? Shall we stop short at the Kantian word – a moral definition of an imagined future, or continue to the Hobbesian realities and look for an objective, geopolitical definition of our joint tomorrow?

The advent of AI, including quantum physics, nanorobotics, and bioinformatics, presents a new and largely unexplored challenge. The potential obsolescence of human physical and mental powers looms on the horizon, raising the question of human relevance in the face of advancing technology.

Humanity is on the brink of a profound redefinition of life itself. The once clear boundary between organic and inorganic, intrinsic and artificial, has been forever blurred.

Although life remains to be lived forward (with no backwards looking), human retrospection is the largest reservoir of insights. Of what makes us human.

Thus, what does the history of technology in relation to human development tell us so far?

Elaborating on a well-known argument of Fukuyama's 'defensive modernization,' it is evident that throughout human history, a technological drive was aimed at satisfying the security and control objective. It was rarely (if at all) driven by a desire to gain knowledge outside of convention to ease human existence and bolster human emancipation and liberation of societies at large. Therefore, unless operationalized by the system, intellectualism (human autonomy, proficiency, and purpose) and technological breakthroughs were traditionally perceived as a threat. As a problem, not a solution.

Cyber-social networks and search engines differ significantly from how they are commonly portrayed: a decentralized but unified intelligence attracted by the gravity of quality rather than navigated by the force of a specific locality.

They do not correspond with the neuroplasticity of the physics of our consciousness. They only offer temporary relaxation to our anxieties – in which the fear of free time is the greatest. It is so since accurate free time coupled with silence is our gate to creativity and self-reflection. The cyber-tools of these data sponges primarily serve purposes of predictability, efficiency, calculability, and control purpose, and only then do they serve everything else – as to be, e.g., user-friendly and end mass service attractive.

The cyber-social platforms- these spaces of social disconnection and emotional desensitization- are particularly interesting in observing the new corrosive dynamics of social phenomenology between manipulative fetishization (probability) and self-trivialization (possibility).

This is how human presence-eliminating technologies have been introduced to and accepted by us.

The international community is acutely aware of the pressing need to develop a new social contract to effectively address the disruptive potential of new technologies, particularly AI. The time for action is now. The deep fakes, dark web, polarizing content, and swarms of bots are expanding all over the cyberspace. The symbiotic relationship between AI and our data-driven society has shifted the majority of our societal interactions to the digital realm. These new masters AI, and data, are already reshaping the very fabric of our realities, underscoring the urgent need for a multilateral approach to AI governance.

No wonder our common anxieties are rising. Are we losing control of the algorithmic revolution of nanorobots? Is AI escaping our traditional modes of understanding and collective action? Public confidence in national governance and global leadership is waning, potentially increasing the risk of social unrest.

Simultaneously, AI-powered nano-, bio-, and info-technological technologies will tend to weaken rather than enforce global and regional governance mechanisms.

AI is a dual-use technology. Its mighty implications (either positive or negative) will be increasingly complex to anticipate, frame, restrain, or mitigate and regulate. The so-called deep fake is a good example. Advanced algorithmic AI programs have reached the stage to easily alter or even manufacture audio and video images by creating impersonations that are practically identical to their original. Deep-learning facial recognition algorithms can already, with astonishing accuracy, copy eye motion, trace, and simulate a variety of facial expressions or even synthesize speech by analyzing breathing patterns in combination with a movement of tongue and lips.

Once released by a state or non-state actor, such artificial interventions could be easily used for a wide range of impacts: political campaigns, racketeering, peer pressures and extortive mobbing. It is not hard to imagine such a fake video triggering public panic (e.g., if it displays non-existent epidemics or cyberattacks), mass demonstrations (e.g., if it portrays a high-ranking official in a bribing scene or similar grave crime), or forged security incidents that may provoke serious international escalations.

The ever-growing number of actors and their increasing capacitation to influence citizens with doctored simulations could pose long-lasting detrimental implications for the UN and other International fora's dealing with peace and security. By corrupting the very notion of truth and of mutual confidence between the citizenry and their state and among states, the deep fakes may become the most significant disruptive force to our global governing system.

Due to advancements in the Internet of Things (IoT), AI is already bridging and coupling with a range of other technologies, especially with the metadata provided by Biotech. These mergers pose a significant challenge to global security. Driven by lucrative commercial prospects or state security considerations, AI systems worldwide are primarily programmed towards the predictability of human behavior. Quite at a reach, they already have accurate and speedy analytics of urban traffic patterns, financial markets, consumer behavior, health records and even our genomes.

These AI technologies are increasingly able to channel our behavioral and biological data in an entirely novel and somewhat manipulative way, with implications for all of us. Neither this spares the youngest among us. For instance, the i-Que boys' robot or Cayla girls' doll transmits voice and emotional data of kids interacting with them (of everyone in their 10-meter proximity radius) and sends it back to their manufacturers via the Cloud. This feature led the European authorities to examine automated toys closely and conclude that they violate basic principles of consumer and privacy protection. Similar dolls are still in extensive use all over the Arab world and Asia, where consumer protection awareness is slower or less organized than in the EU.

In several OECD countries, the deployment of emotional analysis in courtrooms is seriously discussed. In such a scenario, the robust algorithmic biometrics would measure a level of remorse when witnesses are testifying and audio-video materials are presented. If once operable, that would then be easily extended by granting companies the ability to utilize different types of biometrics in assessing job applicants.

That may finally tempt some outcast regimes to force biometric bracelets upon part or even entire populations and have a real-time and accurate measuring of the popular support they enjoy. (Such bracelets are already heavily advocated in some OECD countries for the prison population, especially for re-convalescent inmates charged with serious crimes.

Finally, if the human individual or group behaviors can be monitored, hoovered, processed, and altered, who (or what) will be a driver of electability - a change (or status quo, for that matter) – people or algorithms? If the entire biometrics, emotional data and past behavioristic history of all parliamentarians, all political parties' protagonists, top military, and the key business people is hackable by the national or foreign state or non-state actors – then the sense of democracy, military affairs, security, and human rights will be changed beyond recognition. Most probably, beyond return, too.

Suppose AI has the potential to penetrate – and even steer – individual and group human behaviors. In that case, it inevitably disrupts the very notion of human rights as embedded in the UN Human Rights Charter, as well as of peace, security, prosperity, and equality among states as stipulated by the Charter.

New means of social and biometric control will inevitably necessitate us to revisit and reimage the framework currently in place to monitor and implement the Universal Declaration of Human Rights. This also includes the right to independence and inalienable access to economic development. This will require a concerted effort from regional developmental FORAs and the UN as a universal multilateral system to anticipate and adjust.

The AI is a theatre for future conflicts and new forms of transnational crimes. Since it reduces jobs in their numbers, configurations, and intensities due to automation, AI is excellently suited for the countries in demographic transition (decline) rather than for the booming demographics of the Muslim world, sub-Saharan Africa and (non-Fareast) Asia. Dramatic shrinking in domestic labor conjecture and forthcoming shifts in global manufacturing dependences will especially hit hard in the Global South. Often enveloped in the 'wait-and-see' stance, the Global South traditionally has a low trust rate between its citizenry and government.

Logically, the 'promise of the AI' to sway large regions and their populations is so immediate that it already puts its main drivers to fierce competition. Accelerating competition (with such a disruptive technology) without cooperation or comprehensive regulation is only one step from conflict.

The science fiction-like prospects of ruling the 'AI race,' thus, are becoming realistic: Powerful state or commercial (technology platforms) actors bitterly competing over our collective data – as a new cyber currency – to aggregate bio-medical, economic, and politico-military supremacy across the globe. The "cyber-colonization" – especially of the global South - is increasingly likely. (Hoovering data for free and monetizing it without warning, data-collection taxation, or remuneration to its proprietor.) Leaders in the AI field are already capable of hoovering data globally, have storing capacities, and will soon master (quantum) computing powers to process, analyze, and potentially control other countries' populations and ecosystems.

Quite disturbingly, our societies need to prepare for the deployment of AI: Be it philosophically or practically, we still need thorough socio-political, legal, or ethical considerations. Moreover, the UN and its Agencies – architecture 75 years before the emergence of these technologies – are poorly equipped to offer comprehensive and timely AI governance in many aspects. The speed of this technological innovation cycle outpaces any administrative response, even as the technological disruptions are becoming apparent to more countries.

The new political trends of autarchic 'neo-nationalism' are further trivializing the capacity of the multilateral FORAs to play a norm-setting and monitoring-of-compliance role in the global governance of AI. In such a climate, technologically advanced member states (pressured by their national security or commercial interests) may see little incentive to let the international FORAs govern what they perceive as their own lucrative and proprietary technology.

With all this in mind, the UN, and its Specialized Agencies (including the International Telecommunication Union[13], UNESCO and UN University) and various regional FORAs hold the answer. That very much includes the developmental segments – especially of the global South – such as the African, Asian, Interamerican or Islamic Development Banks, as well as regional politico-administrative settings like the Organization of Islamic Cooperation (OIC)[14], South Asian Association for Regional Cooperation (SAARC)[15], and ASEAN, to name but a few. They must initiate and navigate their member states and steer the world through the universal UN bodies.

Letting the AI train pass without a collective, collaborative form of governance would be a double irreversible setback: Disruptive dual-use technology and digital ownership would be handed over to an alienated few to govern it. At the same time, the trust in a multilateral system (especially within the developing world) would further deteriorate.

---

[13] International Telecommunication Union (ITU), "Committed to Connecting the World," accessed November 24, 2024, https://www.itu.int/es/Pages/default.aspx.

[14] Organization of Islamic Cooperation (OIC), "The Collective Voice of the Muslim World," accessed December 16, 2024, https://www.oic-oci.org/.

[15] South Asian Association for Regional Cooperation (SAARC), accessed September 30, 2024, https://saarc-sec.org/.

We need an accurate, just, and timely multilateral approach to the three gravest planetary challenges (technology, ecology, and nuclear annihilation). Everyone has their share of historical (generational) responsibility in this struggle for relevance.

Criminal organizations are increasingly harnessing artificial intelligence to perpetrate crimes such as identity theft, fraud, and advanced cyberattacks. The incorporation of AI allows these groups to automate operations, analyze large datasets, and conduct attacks with greater efficiency and precision. Moreover, there are rising concerns that AI could orchestrate new forms of criminal activity, leading to situations where AI systems are directly employed in committing crimes or facilitating illicit operations. As these technologies continue to advance, it is crucial for legal frameworks to evolve in tandem, ensuring that responses to cybercrime effectively address the unique challenges posed by the misuse of artificial intelligence

We may be facing an entirely new world, and leaders are fully aware of our challenges. Therefore, there are numerous responses from states and international organizations to regulate the potential risks of artificial intelligence. Among these efforts, a significant step has been taken with the adoption of a Council of Europe Convention on AI systems[16]. This treaty addresses the regulation of AI in both the public and private sectors, reflecting the urgency and complexity of managing AI's impact on society.

The Convention offers parties two ways to comply with its principles and obligations: they can either directly adhere to the convention's provisions or implement alternative measures that align with their international obligations regarding human rights, democracy, and the rule of law. This dual approach is crucial, as it acknowledges the diverse legal systems around the world.

Central to the Convention are its transparency and oversight requirements. Parties are mandated to implement measures to identify, assess, prevent, and mitigate risks associated with AI. This includes evaluating the need for moratoriums or bans on AI applications that could potentially conflict with human rights standards. Additionally, the Convention insists on the identification of AI-generated content to ensure transparency.

The treaty also emphasizes accountability and equality. It requires AI systems to respect human rights, including gender equality and privacy rights, and prohibits discrimination. To safeguard these principles, parties must

---

[16] Council of Europe, Committee of Ministers, Council of Europe Framework Convention on Artificial Intelligence and Human Rights, Democracy, and the Rule of Law, CETS No. 25 (May 17, 2024).

provide legal remedies for individuals adversely affected by AI and ensure procedural safeguards, such as informing people when they are interacting with AI systems.

In terms of protecting democratic values, the Convention mandates that AI should not undermine democratic institutions and processes. This includes upholding the separation of powers, judicial independence, and access to justice. Furthermore, while the Convention does not apply to activities related to national security or defense, it does require that these activities respect international law and democratic principles.

To ensure the effective implementation of these measures, the Convention establishes a follow-up mechanism through a Conference of the Parties. Additionally, each party is required to create an independent oversight mechanism. This body will oversee compliance, raise public awareness, stimulate informed public debate, and engage in consultations on the ethical use of AI technology

The adoption of the Council of Europe Convention on AI systems represents a major milestone in the global effort to manage the risks and harness the benefits of artificial intelligence. At the same time, it highlights the pressing need for a comprehensive international framework - such as a potential United Nations convention - that can address the complex and evolving challenges posed by AI. In the absence of such global governance, there is a real danger that the inequalities and threats amplified by AI technologies will remain unchecked, deepening existing disparities and fueling instability. As we move forward in this rapidly changing landscape, it is essential that nations work together to establish robust regulatory frameworks that prioritize ethical principles, safeguard individual rights, and foster public trust in technological progress.

5.3. Environmental Crimes

Environmental crime is one of the fastest-growing global challenges we face today. What makes it even harder to tackle is that there isn't a universally agreed-upon definition of it. This lack of clarity creates gaps in the system - gaps that organized criminal groups are quick to exploit. As these crimes become more frequent and more destructive, the consequences go far beyond damaged ecosystems. They threaten people's health, livelihoods, and the well-being of future generations.

There are serious offenses - like illegal logging, toxic waste dumping, and wildlife trafficking - that cause lasting harm. However, the issue extends beyond these offenses. Environmental crimes are often part of something bigger. They're tied to money laundering, corruption, identity theft, and sometimes even violence. These networks are smart, well-funded, and they take advantage of weak laws, poorly resourced authorities, and the fact that countries do not always work well together.

The environmental and societal impact is considerable. Endangered animals are being driven to extinction in some parts of the world. Forests are being cleared illegally, leading to soil erosion and exacerbating the climate crisis. Hazardous waste is poisoning rivers and groundwater, putting whole communities at risk.

Addressing this issue requires more than prosecuting individual offenders; it is about global teamwork. We need a common definition of environmental crime, stronger laws, better enforcement, and more cooperation between countries.

Recognizing the factors that reinforce the nexus between corruption and environmental crimes, including tax burdens, excessive regulation of legal markets, bureaucratic hurdles, and high public spending, is crucial.

National and transnational crime networks emerge as significant actors in environmental offenses, leveraging their control over public resources and influence within local, regional, and national governmental institutions. Exploiting circumstances characterized by a notable degree of moral acceptance and weak governance structures, these criminal organizations take advantage of vulnerabilities in authorization systems. Furthermore, the legal approach to environmental crimes often adopts a formalistic stance, focusing on punitive legislation irrespective of the environmental harm caused, thereby facilitating the link between environmental crimes and corruption.

Moreover, the intricate nature of environmental crimes, which often intertwine with various forms of organized crime, adds a layer of complexity to their identification and accurate reporting. This complexity, in turn, makes it challenging to isolate and report organized environmental offenses within the broader spectrum of crime statistics.

The interconnections between environmental crimes and organized crimes, particularly evident in activities such as wildlife trafficking, transnational trafficking in waste, and illegal logging, highlight the urgent need to raise awareness about these connections. However, the absence of a universally recognized definition of environmental crime hampers international efforts to effectively address these issues. The lack of an international legal instrument to respond to environmental crimes further complicates the situation. Therefore, establishing and enforcing international legal mechanisms at the national level is essential to implement international environmental law and combat these illegal activities, which present challenges for law enforcement and implementation, including Multilateral Environmental Agreements (MEAs). The promotion of environmental democracy through engagement in environmental justice, with local communities, NGOs, and civil societies playing pivotal and empowering roles, is crucial in this context.

Stepping beyond conventional understandings, reaching a consensus on an internationally recognized definition is of utmost importance. This necessitates collective efforts to develop a framework that empowers UN member states to enhance cooperation in law enforcement and bridge gaps in understanding and action. With a clear definition, the fight against environmental crime will be bolstered by adequate resource allocation and political prioritization, despite the enforcement challenges. This underscores the crucial role of each entity in this global issue.

Furthermore, states need more understanding and coordination regarding this relatively new category of transnational crimes. Internationally coordinated efforts and enhanced law enforcement cooperation are indispensable in addressing this gap. However, the lack of adequate funding further exacerbates the challenges faced by actors combating environmental crimes, who are often under-resourced compared to well-funded criminal entities.

This significant disparity in financial means enables criminals to exploit the environment for monetary gain at the expense of its preservation. Against this context, Interpol remains a crucial source of criminal intelligence in combating environmental crimes[17]. Addressing these issues requires concerted efforts at both national and international levels to effectively combat environmental crimes and their interconnectedness with organized criminal activities.

Trafficking and illegal dumping of hazardous waste pose a multifaceted challenge with significant implications. Illegal activities extend beyond mere waste dumping to transportation and landfill management in violation of international or domestic legal provisions. This poses a significant threat to public health and the environment and contributes to social and economic instability.

---

[17] Ibid.

The low risk of prosecution and lenient sentencing have transformed hazardous waste disposal into a lucrative business opportunity for criminal networks. Organized crime organizations operate in well-structured networks, facilitating the illegal disposal of hazardous waste.

To maximize profits, an increasing number of legal enterprises engage in waste trafficking or illegal dumping through intermediaries, exploiting regulatory loopholes that make circumventing the system more cost-effective than compliance.

The escalating production of hazardous waste, particularly electronic waste, exacerbates the transboundary movement of such materials, affecting both major producing and importing countries. The link between criminal activities and the illegal trade of electronic waste presents challenges due to vague regulatory frameworks. Corruption among public officials responsible for permits, law enforcement, customs, and politicians further facilitate waste trafficking by enabling the evasion of bureaucratic hurdles.

The rise in illegal trade between the European Union and severely affected destination countries in Africa and Asia distorts market competition, forcing legitimate waste disposal firms to lower prices and compromise service quality to remain competitive. This underscores the urgent need for robust regulatory frameworks and international cooperation to combat illegal waste trafficking and promote responsible waste management practices.

At the international level, the United Nations has implemented significant measures to address transnational environmental crimes, guided by Resolution 10/6 of October 16, 2020[18]. This resolution, titled "Preventing and Combating Crimes that Affect the Environment within the Scope of the United Nations Convention against Transnational Organized Crime," mandates collaborative efforts to apply the UNTOC to environmental crimes.

In May 2022, the Working Group on International Cooperation and the Working Group of Government Experts on Technical Assistance convened to discuss these issues. It adopted several recommendations to enhance the Convention's application in this area. They advocated classifying environmental crimes as severe offenses under national laws to facilitate international cooperation. Additionally, they proposed treating these crimes as predicate offenses for money laundering, thereby improving financial

[18] United Nations Office on Drugs and Crime, Resolution 10/6: Preventing and Combating Crimes that Affect the Environment Falling within the Scope of the United Nations Convention against Transnational Organized Crime (October 16, 2020).

investigations and enabling the seizure of assets from organized criminal groups involved in environmental crimes.

The recommendations emphasized the necessity of stronger international cooperation and information sharing on the connections between environmental crimes and other forms of organized crime.

The use of technology was also promoted to enhance law enforcement cooperation, joint investigations, extradition, and mutual legal assistance. Addressing the challenges posed by the double criminality principle, the recommendations called for ensuring that the conduct underlying environmental crimes is criminalized in both the requesting and requested states, regardless of how the crime is categorized or named. And anti-corruption measures were deemed essential, with states urged to leverage the Palermo Convention and the UN Convention against Corruption to combat corruption that facilitates these crimes.

The UNODC was tasked with continuing its support for states through technical assistance and capacity-building. Furthermore, the UNODC was encouraged to collect data and research environmental crimes using the SHERLOC knowledge management portal[19]. Despite these efforts, addressing organized environmental crime remains challenging due to this field's lack of legal and criminal policy traditions. The Green Customs Initiative[20], launched in 2004, aims to enhance the capacity of customs and border control officers to monitor and prevent illegal trade in environmentally sensitive products, involving partners such as INTERPOL, UNEP[21], and the World Customs Organization. The Timber Regulation and the UN Minamata Convention [22]also aim to prevent environmental damage from timber trade and mercury usage, respectively. From 30 December 2024 the Timber Regulation (EU) 995/2010 will be replaced by the new Regulation (EU) 2023/1115 (EUDR) on deforestation and forest degradation with much more products in its scope. The Aarhus Convention[23] establishes rules on access to justice and

---

[19] United Nations Office on Drugs and Crime,, "Sharing Electronic Resources and Laws on Crime (SHERLOC)," accessed November 24, 2024, https://sherloc.unodc.org/cld/en/st/home.html.

[20] Green Customs, "The Green Customs Initiative," accessed November 24, 2024, https://www.greencustoms.org/.

[21] United Nations Environment Programme (UNEP), "Who We Are, Where We Work, What We Do," accessed November 24, 2024, https://www.unep.org/.

[22] United Nations General Assembly, Minamata Convention on Mercury (October 10, 2013).

[23] United Nations General Assembly, Convention on Access to Information, Public Participation in Decision-Making and Access to Justice in Environmental Matters (Aarhus, June 25, 1998).

environmental matters, but challenges remain in public participation, victim awareness, and proving and quantifying environmental damage.

International conventions like the Palermo Convention, Basel Convention[24], and Bamako Convention[25] provide legal frameworks to identify and regulate hazardous materials and environmental crimes. These Conventions emphasize the need for harmonizing efforts and improving institutional collaboration among different agencies and stakeholders to address the transnational nature of environmental crimes.

Cooperation with international and regional organizations, NGOs, the private sector, and other stakeholders was also encouraged to prevent and combat environmental crimes and raise awareness. Specifically, measures to combat wildlife trafficking were highlighted, urging states to consider the impact of trafficking in wildlife in all involved countries.

Overall, the UN's initiatives against environmental crimes focus on strengthening legal frameworks, enhancing international cooperation, and leveraging technology to address these complex issues on a global scale effectively.

At the regional level, there has been a special common regulation at the European Union level. The European Union has also sought to tackle environmental crimes, though the issue remains complex and multifaceted. Despite having the authority to harmonize environmental criminal law, the EU faces challenges such as the unclear relationship between organized crime and environmental law, and ambiguities in the interplay between criminal and administrative laws in the environmental sector.

Sanctions for environmental crimes vary across EU member states, and there are no specific EU-level sanctions. Complementary sanctions can be applied, but this practice needs to be more consistent. Nonetheless, the EU emphasizes Corporate Social Responsibility[26], holding companies and their management accountable for transparent and responsible business behavior. Directive 2014/95/EU[27] mandates binding disclosure requirements for large

---

[24] United Nations General Assembly, The Basel Convention on the Control of Transboundary Movements of Hazardous Wastes and Their Disposal (March 22, 1989).

[25] Bamako Convention on the Ban of the Import into Africa and the Control of Transboundary Movement and Management of Hazardous Wastes within Africa, adopted by 51 African countries, Bamako, Mali, January 30, 1991, entered into force April 22, 1998.

[26] European Union, Directive 2022/2464 of the European Parliament and of the Council of December 14, 2022, Amending Regulation No. 537/2014, Directive 2004/109/EC, Directive 2006/43/EC, and Directive 2013/34/EU, as Regards Corporate Sustainability Reporting.

[27] European Union, Directive 2014/95/EU of the European Parliament and of the Council of October 22, 2014, Amending Directive 2013/34/EU as Regards Disclosure of Non-

companies, covering environmental protection, social responsibility, human rights, anti-corruption measures, and board diversity. This Directive aims to enhance corporate accountability and transparency, indirectly contributing to efforts against environmental crime.

Voluntary professional associations share information and best practices, but many environmental crimes remain to be yet investigated due to a limited awareness, complexity, and resource constraints. Member states are not obligated to report ongoing investigations to EUROPOL and EUROJUST, hindering cross-border cooperation. Environmental democracy is promoted through engagement in environmental justice, with local communities, NGOs, and civil societies playing crucial roles.

The EU is a member of several multilateral environmental agreements and has expertise in tools, networks, and enforcement agencies for both EU and transnational cases. EU enforcement networks operate at national and transnational levels, and the EU funds efforts to combat wildlife crime.

Supporting legislation and agreements, such as Directive 2008/99/EC[28] on Environmental Crime, the Ship-Source Pollution Directive[29], provide legal frameworks to combat environmental crime. EU legislation, including Article 83(1) and (2) of the Treaty on the Functioning of the European Union[30] (TFEU), permits the establishment of minimum standards for defining criminal offenses and penalties. Directive 2014/95/EU[31] mandates corporate disclosure requirements regarding environmental protection, social responsibility, and anti-corruption measures. A new Environmental Crime Directive (2024/1203[32]) was adopted on 11 April 2024 and entered into force on 20 May 2024, supporting the protection of the environment through

---

Financial and Diversity Information by Certain Large Undertakings and Groups, OJ L 330 (November 15, 2014): 1–9.

[28] European Union, Directive 2008/99/EC of the European Parliament and of the Council of November 19, 2008, on the Protection of the Environment through Criminal Law (Text with EEA Relevance), OJ L 328 (December 6, 2008): 28–37.

[29] European Union, Directive 2005/35/EC of the European Parliament and of the Council of September 7, 2005, on Ship-Source Pollution and on the Introduction of Penalties for Infringements, OJ L 255 (September 30, 2005): 11–21.

[30] European Union Conference of the Representatives of the Governments of the Member States, Consolidated Version of the Treaty on the Functioning of the European Union, 2008/C 115/01 (December 13, 2007).

[31] European Union, Directive 2014/95/EU Amending Directive 2013/34/EU as Regards Disclosure of Non-Financial and Diversity Information by Certain Large Undertakings and Groups (October 22, 2014).

[32] European Union, Directive (EU) 2024/1203 of the European Parliament and of the Council of April 11, 2024, on the Protection of the Environment through Criminal Law, OJ L 2024/1203 (April 30, 2024).

criminal law and replacing the 2008/99 Environmental Crime Directive. This new Directive requires EU member states to classify serious breaches of environmental regulations as criminal offenses within their national laws, ensuring consistency in enforcement across the Union.

The Directive introduces new offense categories, such as unlawful ship recycling, illegal water abstraction, and significant violations related to EU chemicals, mercury, fluorinated greenhouse gases, and invasive alien species. It mandates stricter penalties for offenses causing severe, widespread, and substantial environmental damage, enhancing the deterrent effect.

Additionally, the Directive standardizes penalties for both individuals and organizations, and includes provisions to strengthen the enforcement chain. This ensures that practitioners combating environmental crimes have sufficient resources and training, and provides support for environmental defenders during criminal proceedings.

Despite all international efforts, there is still a long way to go. The environment is undoubtedly one of the greatest challenges we face today, and courageous action is also needed to tackle transnational organized crime affecting the environment. Enhancing transparency in public permit and access-granting systems can reduce the influence of organized crime networks. Positive incentives, like establishing recycling facilities and markets for recycled materials, can help manage hazardous waste production. Implementing stricter penalties can dissuade individuals from engaging in criminal activities. Investigating related crimes, particularly e-waste trade, is necessary to understand the extent of criminal activities. Collaborative efforts are essential in addressing human rights abuses and exploitation associated with environmental crimes. Enforcing competition rules can curb the influence of criminal networks, promoting fair competition and reducing their market manipulation.

Identifying gaps and barriers is crucial for developing effective solutions to environmental crimes. Efforts should focus on preventing such crimes through linked legislation and enhancing cooperation among agencies and stakeholders. An internationally recognized definition of environmental crime is necessary, as the current understanding needs more clarity. Mechanisms to bridge the gap between environmental crimes and corruption, such as information systems for monitoring, are essential. Simplifying market regulations, increasing transparency, and initiating discussions on legal approaches can mitigate corruption, which often facilitates environmental crimes.

5.4. Biohacking

Biohacking is a rapidly growing movement that involves manipulating biological systems - whether through self-experimentation, diet, or advanced technologies such as genetic modification — to enhance physical and mental performance. While the practice ranges from simple adjustments to far more radical interventions like implanting devices or modifying one's DNA, and it raises significant legal and ethical concerns, particularly in the context of transnational crime. This unregulated landscape creates opportunities for exploitation, where biohacking practices can lead to criminal actions that exploit regulatory gaps across borders.

With its rise, biohacking is challenging traditional legal and ethical boundaries, especially in the European Union, where regulations concerning health, technology and data privacy are highly developed.

While biohacking promises revolutionary changes in how individuals control and enhance their bodies, it also sits on the fringes of legality, often exploiting regulatory gaps. Biohackers in the EU may face restrictions under treaties like the Oviedo Convention[33] or national laws governing human experimentation, but many aspects of biohacking remain unregulated or loosely controlled.

In traditional dictionaries, it is often portrayed as a narrow and sometimes controversial practice. The Cambridge Dictionary defines biohacking[34] as "scientific experiments with biological material, especially genes, done by people who are not official experts or scientists, either as a hobby or in order to make money or commit crime." This definition emphasizes biohacking's potential for risk and unconventional methods of biological manipulation. Similarly, Merriam-Webster describes it as "biological experimentation (as by gene editing or the use of drugs or implants) done to improve the qualities or capabilities of living organisms, especially by individuals and groups operating outside traditional medical or scientific research environments"[35]. This perspective reflects biohacking as a self-directed, experimental practice usually conducted beyond conventional scientific settings. Biohacking may

---

33 Council of Europe, *Convention for the Protection of Human Rights and Dignity of the Human Being with regard to the Application of Biology and Medicine: Convention on Human Rights and Biomedicine*, Oviedo, April 4, 1997. Accessed November 24, 2024. https://rm.coe.int/168007cf98.

34 Cambridge Dictionary, s.v. "biohacking," accessed November 24, 2024, https://dictionary.cambridge.org/dictionary/english/biohacking.

35 Merriam-Webster.com Dictionary, s.v. "biohacking," accessed November 24, 2024, https://www.merriam-webster.com/dictionary/biohacking.

also be conceptualized as externally induced, concealed gene intervention for the non-transparent ends (author's proposed definition).

Biohacking has evolved into a form of "DIY (do it yourself) biology," where individuals - often outside institutional frameworks - apply biological science and technology to optimize their bodies and biological systems. According to Meyer[36], biohacking thrives in peer production environments where knowledge and resources are openly shared, allowing individuals to take control of their biology through accessible tools, including wearable devices, supplements, and even genetic modification. This approach reflects a democratization of science that disrupts traditional boundaries between professional and amateur scientists, raising ethical concerns around safety, privacy and regulation[37].

As a grassroots movement, biohacking blends biology with principles of open science and DIY experimentation. Delfanti [38] suggests that biohacking challenges conventional scientific hierarchies by emphasizing collaboration and open access to biological knowledge and tools. Biohackers frequently conduct experiments to push the limits of human biology, promoting a democratized science culture. This movement advocates for peer production and low-cost technologies as a form of resistance against proprietary, closed scientific systems.

Broadly, biohacking encompasses various practices aimed at modifying or optimizing human biology. Techniques range from simple lifestyle changes, such as dietary adjustments, to advanced interventions like genetic modification and the implantation of technological devices. Biohacking integrates diverse life sciences techniques beyond the confines of traditional academic and corporate research, further blurring the lines between professional and amateur scientists[39].

While many biohacking techniques are health-focused, others pursue aesthetic, psychological, or even transhumanist objectives, exploring the extension of human capabilities through technology.

---

[36] M. Meyer, "Biohacking," in *The Handbook of Peer Production*, eds. M. O'Neil, C. Pentzold, and S. Toupin (Malden, MA: Wiley-Blackwell, 2020), 211–224. ISBN 9781119537106. Accessed November 24, 2024. https://www.wiley.com/en-au/The+Handbook+of+Peer+Production-p-9781119537090.

[37] Ibid.

[38] Alessandro Delfanti, *Biohackers: The Politics of Open Science* (Cambridge: Polity, 2013). Accessed November 24, 2024. https://delfanti.org/biohackers/.

[39] Christopher Coenen, "Biohacking: New Do-It-Yourself Practices as Technoscientific Work between Freedom and Necessity," *Proceedings* 1, no. 3 (2017): 256.

5.4.1. Lifestyle Optimization

This form of biohacking focuses on enhancing well-being through manageable interventions in daily life. Key practices include improving diet, sleep, exercise, and stress management. Tools such as wearable devices (e.g., fitness trackers) are used to monitor biomarkers, sleep quality, and heart rate, allowing individuals to make informed decisions about their health. Simple interventions like intermittent fasting, cold exposure, and natural supplements fall under this category[40]. Mental enhancement is a significant focus within the field of biohacking, which encompasses a variety of methods aimed at improving cognitive function, emotional regulation, and mental resilience. Biohackers seek to optimize their mental capabilities by utilizing a range of tools and techniques, such as nootropics, mindfulness practices, neurostimulation and targeted lifestyle interventions. Nootropics, also known as cognitive enhancers or "smart drugs," are substances that may improve various aspects of brain function, including memory, focus and executive function. Caffeine and L-theanine, commonly found in tea, are widely used and extensively studied nootropics[41]. When combined, these compounds have been shown to enhance cognitive performance by improving attention and reducing mental fatigue[42]. Another example is modafinil, a prescription medication typically used to treat sleep disorders, which has been shown to enhance attention, executive function and memory in both clinical and healthy populations[43]

5.4.2. Do-it-yourself Biology (DIY)

DIY biology represents a more experimental branch of biohacking, often involving community labs where enthusiasts use biological tools and techniques typically reserved for professional researchers. Examples include genetic manipulation, open-source insulin production (as in the Open Insulin

---

[40] Ibid.

[41] Chanaka N. Kahathuduwa et al., "Acute Effects of Theanine, Caffeine and Theanine–Caffeine Combination on Attention," *Nutritional Neuroscience* 20, no. 6 (2016): 369–377.

[42] Ibid.

[43] R. M. Battleday and A.-K. Brem, "Modafinil for Cognitive Neuroenhancement in Healthy Non-Sleep-Deprived Subjects: A Systematic Review," *European Neuropsychopharmacology* 25, no. 11 (2015): 1865–1881.

Project[44]), or developing personalized medical treatments. These practices emphasize democratizing biotechnology, making advanced tools accessible outside academic or corporate labs[45]. One of the primaries uses of DIYbio is in genetic engineering, where individuals can experiment with organisms, such as bacteria or yeast, to modify genetic material. This could include projects like creating fluorescent bacteria or altering plants to produce new compounds. Meyer notes that technologies such as CRISPR (Clustered Regularly Interspaced Short Palindromic Repeats) have made gene editing more accessible to non-professional scientists, allowing for experimentation with genetic material at a relatively low cost[46].

5.4.3. Grinders and Transhumanism

At the extreme end of the biohacking spectrum are individuals known as "grinders" or DIY transhumanists. These biohackers embrace invasive procedures, including the implantation of electronic devices (such as microchips) to enhance sensory capabilities or monitor health data. Their goal is often to transcend biological limits, entering the realm of cyborgs. Ethical and regulatory concerns are prevalent in this area due to the experimental and sometimes dangerous nature of these modifications[47]. Grinders push the boundaries of self-experimentation, using devices such as RFID chips for unlocking doors, magnets implanted in fingertips for sensing electromagnetic fields, or even more advanced biotechnologies aimed at enhancing sensory perception or communication capabilities. Fuisz emphasizes the lack of legal frameworks to address the potential risks or unintended consequences of these experiments. This absence of regulation presents both an opportunity for innovation and a potential hazard, as these practices exist outside the traditional boundaries of medical and scientific research [48].

---

[44] Open Insulin Foundation, "Open Insulin Foundation," accessed November 24, 2024, https://openinsulin.org/.

[45] The Medical Futurist, "The Current State and Future of Biohacking," 2024. Accessed November 24, 2024. https://medicalfuturist.com/the-current-state-and-future-of-biohacking/.

[46] The Medical Futurist, "The Current State and Future of Biohacking," 2024. Accessed November 24, 2024. https://medicalfuturist.com/the-current-state-and-future-of-biohacking/.

[47] M. Meyer, "Biohacking," in *The Handbook of Peer Production*, eds. M. O'Neil, C. Pentzold, and S. Toupin (Malden, MA: Wiley-Blackwell, 2020), 211–224.

[48] Christopher Coenen, "Biohacking: New Do-It-Yourself Practices as Technoscientific Work between Freedom and Necessity," *Proceedings* 1, no. 3 (2017): 256.

5.4.4. Ethical and Regulatory Considerations

The rapid rise of biohacking has sparked debates about its safety and the ethical implications of self-experimentation. While many biohackers claim that their efforts help to advance health technologies, this movement often operates under conditions where activities may cross into criminal activities. The lack of adequate regulatory oversight presents a significant risk, enabling potential transnational crime related to unauthorized genetic modifications, health fraud, and the exploitation of vulnerable individuals.

For example, invasive body modifications raise concerns about safety, legality and the potential for misuse. On the other hand, biohacking movements like DIY biology advocate for open access to scientific tools, which may contribute to more affordable healthcare solutions, such as producing cheaper medications like insulin[49].

Currently, the tension between innovation and regulation in biohacking is highly discussed. Too much regulation might stifle creativity and personal freedom, but too little might lead to widespread harm. The challenge is to strike a balance that allows biohackers to innovate while protecting public safety and ethical standards. This raises the question of whether new laws and regulations should be created specifically for biohacking, or whether existing medical and scientific frameworks are sufficient to address these concerns[50]

The rapid growth of biohacking, particularly in DIY biology and personal health modification, has raised complex legal and ethical challenges within the EU and beyond, highlighting the need for international cooperation in regulation. While biohacking itself is not explicitly addressed by a singular legal framework, its various practices intersect with numerous existing EU regulations, which must adapt to counteract the potential transnational crime that may arise from these loosely regulated practices, including illegal human experimentation and exploitation across borders.

These frameworks, which govern data protection, medical devices, genetic modification and ethical biomedical research, indirectly regulate biohacking activities. As the line between personal experimentation and formal biomedical innovation blurs, it becomes essential to understand how

---

[49] Richard Fuisz, "Caveat Creator," *Journal of Law and the Biosciences* 4, no. 3 (December 2017): 658–670.

[50] Viterbi Conversations in Ethics, "Biohacking: The Ethical Implications of Democratizing Biotechnology," accessed November 24, 2024. https://vce.usc.edu/volume-5-issue-2/biohacking-the-ethical-implications-of-democratizing-biotechnology/.

EU regulations address the safety, privacy and ethical considerations surrounding this emerging field.

5.4.5. Clinical Trials Regulation (EU) No 536/2014

The Clinical Trials Regulation (Regulation (EU) No 536/2014[51]) sets out specific requirements for conducting clinical trials involving human subjects. Article 28 of this Regulation focuses on informed consent, mandating that participants must be fully informed of the objectives, risks and benefits of the trial before they can participate. For biohackers engaging in any form of human experimentation, particularly in the realm of medical devices or novel health interventions, compliance with this article is essential to ensure that ethical standards are met. Furthermore, Article 35 establishes provisions for vulnerable populations, such as individuals with reduced autonomy, who may be more susceptible to harm from risky biohacking experiments.

5.4.6. Medical Device Regulation (MDR) (Regulation (EU) 2017/745)

The Medical Device Regulation (Regulation (EU) 2017/745[52]) applies to all medical devices placed on the market within the EU, including those used in biohacking activities. Article 2(1) of the MDR defines a medical device as "any instrument, apparatus, appliance, software, implant, reagent, material or other article" intended for medical purposes, such as diagnosis, prevention, or treatment of diseases. This Regulation is relevant to biohackers who develop or modify devices for health enhancement or biomedical experimentation. Additionally, Article 5(1) of the MDR mandates that any device used in a medical context must comply with EU conformity assessment procedures, ensuring that the device is safe, effective and bears a CE marking.

---

[51] European Union, Regulation (EU) No. 536/2014 of the European Parliament and of the Council of April 16, 2014, on Clinical Trials on Medicinal Products for Human Use, and Repealing Directive 2001/20/EC.

[52] European Union, Regulation (EU) 2017/745 of the European Parliament and of the Council of April 5, 2017, on Medical Devices.

5.4.7. Biotechnology Directive

Directive 98/44/EC[53], known as the Biotechnology Directive, governs the legal protection of biotechnological inventions in the EU. Articles 5 and 6 of the Directive directly address the patentability of biotechnological inventions, particularly concerning genetic engineering. Article 5(1) states that "The human body, at the various stages of its formation and development, and the simple discovery of one of its elements, including the sequence or partial sequence of a gene, cannot constitute patentable inventions." However, Article 5(2) allows for the patenting of isolated elements of the human body, such as gene sequences, under specific conditions. This is highly relevant for biohackers involved in genetic editing or modification, as they must ensure compliance with the directive's provisions regarding patent protection and the ethical use of genetic materials.

5.4.8. The Oviedo Convention on Human Rights and Biomedicine

The Oviedo Convention, also known as the Convention for the Protection of Human Rights and Dignity of the Human Being with regard to the Application of Biology and Medicine, is a crucial legal instrument in regulating bioethical issues. While not binding across all EU member states, it establishes ethical principles for biomedical research and medical practices. Article 5 of the Convention outlines the necessity of informed consent in medical interventions, stating that any procedure related to health may only be carried out after the person has been informed and has provided free and informed consent. Article 13 of the Convention prohibits genetic modifications aimed at altering the genome of descendants, thereby setting ethical boundaries on genetic biohacking practices that could affect future generations.

5.4.9. Genetically Modified Organism (GMO) Regulation

For biohackers involved in genetic modification, the Genetically Modified Organism (GMO) Regulation (Regulation (EC) No 1829/2003[54]) is essential.

---

[53] European Union, Directive 98/44/EC of the European Parliament and of the Council of July 6, 1998, on the Legal Protection of Biotechnological Inventions.

[54] European Union, Regulation (EC) No. 1829/2003 of the European Parliament and of the Council of September 22, 2003, on Genetically Modified Food and Feed.

Article 4 of this Regulation sets out requirements for the authorization of GMOs intended for human consumption, while Article 16 requires rigorous risk assessments before any GMOs can be released into the environment. These provisions ensure that biohacking activities involving genetic engineering must meet strict safety standards to protect both public health and the environment. Additionally, Directive 2001/18/EC[55] on the deliberate release of GMOs into the environment mandates a notification and approval process for biohackers intending to experiment with genetically modified organisms outside of controlled laboratory environments.

5.4.10. EU Charter of Fundamental Rights

The EU Charter of Fundamental Rights provides a broader ethical and human rights context that applies to biohacking. Article 1 guarantees human dignity, while Article 3 protects the right to physical and mental integrity, particularly in the context of medical or scientific experimentation. Biohackers must ensure that their practices respect these fundamental rights, especially in cases where human subjects are involved. Article 3 also explicitly prohibits the use of the human body and its parts as a source of financial gain, a provision that could be relevant to biohackers engaging in the commercialization of biotechnological innovations involving the human body.

5.4.11. Regulatory Gaps and Legal Loopholes in Biohacking Regulation in the European Union

While the European Union has implemented a range of regulations that indirectly govern aspects of biohacking - such as the GDPR for data privacy, the Medical Device Regulation (MDR) for devices, and the Biotechnology Directive for genetic modification - these frameworks were not specifically designed with biohacking in mind. As a result, gaps exist in their coverage, particularly around practices like DIY biology, self-experimentation and citizen-led research. For instance, the regulatory scope often fails to account for biohacking activities that occur outside traditional medical or research

---

[55] European Union, Directive 2001/18/EC of the European Parliament and of the Council of March 12, 2001, on the Deliberate Release into the Environment of Genetically Modified Organisms.

institutions, leaving enforcement and oversight in these areas limited. Furthermore, the rapid pace of technological advancement in biohacking often outstrips the adaptability of existing laws, leading to ambiguity in critical areas such as liability, safety standards and ethical boundaries.

5.4.12. Biohacking Outside of Institutional Oversight

One of the primary challenges in regulating biohacking is the distinction between institutional and non-institutional research. EU regulations such as the Clinical Trials Regulation (EU) No 536/2014[56] are designed to oversee formal clinical trials conducted by medical institutions or companies. However, biohacking often occurs in informal or private settings, such as in personal labs or at home, outside the purview of these established oversight mechanisms. This means that individuals engaging in self-experimentation or DIY biology may bypass stringent safety and ethical guidelines required for institutional research, such as informed consent, independent ethics committee approval, and public safety measures.

Moreover, many biohackers operate outside the traditional research funding structures, meaning their activities do not fall under the purview of Horizon Europe[57] or other EU funding programs, which impose strict ethical and regulatory compliance on grant recipients. As a result, a substantial amount of biohacking activity exists in an unregulated space, where enforcement is minimal.

5.4.13. Self-Experimentation and Personal Autonomy

One of the most complex areas of biohacking regulation involves self-experimentation, where individuals modify or enhance their own biological systems. While EU laws such as the Medical Device Regulation (MDR) (Regulation (EU) 2017/745[58]) establish clear standards for the safety and

---

56 European Union, Regulation (EU) No. 536/2014 of the European Parliament and of the Council of April 16, 2014, on Clinical Trials on Medicinal Products for Human Use.

57 European Commission, "Horizon Europe," accessed December 16, 2024, https://research-and-innovation.ec.europa.eu/funding/funding-opportunities/funding-programmes-and-open-calls/horizon-europe_en.

58 European Union, Regulation (EU) 2017/745 of the European Parliament and of the Council on Medical Devices (April 5, 2017).

effectiveness of medical devices, they are primarily intended for commercial products rather than personal use. Biohackers who implant devices in their own bodies or modify their own biological systems may argue that these interventions fall under personal autonomy and bodily integrity, concepts protected by Article 3 of the EU Charter of Fundamental Rights, which guarantees the right to physical and mental integrity.

The loophole here is that self-experimentation may evade scrutiny because biohackers are often both the researchers and the subjects of their own experiments. As long as the devices or modifications are not sold commercially or performed by third parties, these activities may not be subject to strict medical regulation. This creates ambiguity in terms of accountability and risk management, particularly when biohacking results in harm to the individual or unintended consequences for others, such as environmental risks from genetically modified organisms (GMOs).

5.4.14. Ambiguities in Genetic Modification and Biotechnology

Biohacking frequently involves genetic modification, whether through gene editing technologies like CRISPR or synthetic biology. The Biotechnology Directive (Directive 98/44/EC) governs the legal protection of biotechnological inventions but is focused primarily on patent law and intellectual property rather than regulating amateur genetic experimentation. While this Directive addresses the patentability of biotechnological inventions, it offers limited guidance on the regulation of private or hobbyist genetic modification projects, especially those that are not intended for commercial use.

Furthermore, EU GMO regulations, such as Regulation (EC) No 1829/2003[59] and Directive 2001/18/EC[60], require authorization and risk assessment for the release of genetically modified organisms into the environment.

---

[59] European Union, Regulation (EC) No. 1829/2003 of the European Parliament and of the Council on Genetically Modified Food and Feed (September 22, 2003).

[60] European Union, Directive 2001/18/EC of the European Parliament and of the Council on the Deliberate Release into the Environment of Genetically Modified Organisms and Repealing Council Directive 90/220/EEC (March 12, 2001).

5.4.15. Data Privacy and Ethical Challenges

Biohacking often involves the collection of personal health data, whether through implanted sensors, biometric monitoring or genetic testing. The GDPR governs the collection and processing of personal data, including biometric and genetic information. However, biohackers may exploit certain ambiguities in GDPR, particularly when it comes to consent and the use of personal data for self-experimentation or non-commercial purposes.

For instance, Article 9 of the GDPR prohibits the processing of special categories of personal data unless the individual has given explicit consent. In biohacking, where the data subject and the experimenter are often the same person, consent is not as rigorously monitored or enforced as it would be in institutional research. This creates risks in terms of data security, ethical use of personal data and the potential for misuse of sensitive genetic information.

Moreover, biohackers who share data within communities or open-source platforms may inadvertently expose personal health information without adhering to GDPR compliance, particularly when cross-border data transfers are involved.

5.4.16. Legal and Ethical Responsibility for Community-Based Biohacking

Biohacking communities often work collaboratively, sharing knowledge, techniques and even experimental results. These activities, while fostering innovation, also raise questions about responsibility and accountability. If an individual biohacker suffers harm or if a genetically modified organism inadvertently affects the environment, it remains unclear who would bear legal liability. The EU's existing legal frameworks primarily address institutional responsibility (e.g., corporations or research institutions) rather than distributed, decentralized communities of individuals.

As a result, EU regulations struggle to define clear accountability in cases where harm is caused by biohacking activities.

5.4.17. The Need for Evolving Regulatory Mechanisms

While the EU has established a robust legal framework to regulate biotechnology, medical devices and personal data, these regulations were largely designed with formal institutions and commercial enterprises in mind. Biohacking, as a decentralized and often informal practice, exploits several legal loopholes, particularly concerning self-experimentation, private genetic modification, and community-based research. These gaps allow biohackers to operate with minimal oversight, raising concerns about safety, ethical responsibility and the environmental impact of biohacking activities.

Moving forward, policymakers will need to address these regulatory gaps by creating adaptable legal frameworks that account for the unique nature of biohacking. This may involve introducing new rules specific to DIY biology, tightening enforcement mechanisms and clarifying liability in cases of harm or environmental damage. Furthermore, fostering collaboration between biohackers and regulators could help create a balanced approach that encourages innovation while ensuring public safety and ethical standards are upheld.

The legal status of self-experimentation and personal biohacking poses significant challenges within the context of transnational crime, particularly in the EU. The ambiguity surrounding these practices creates regulatory gaps, as individuals who modify their bodies or conduct personal experiments often fall outside established frameworks intended for formal medical research. This lack of clarity can potentially facilitate illicit activities, such as unregulated genetic modifications or the unauthorized use of medical devices, which may cross international borders. To tackle these issues, policymakers should establish specific regulations addressing personal biohacking, especially regarding the use of medical devices and genetic applications, to prevent misuse that could contribute to transnational crime.

Biohacking often occurs outside conventional research settings, with individuals or small groups conducting experiments in private labs or community spaces. This decentralized environment complicates oversight and control, leaving room for activities that may endanger public health and the environment or support illicit objectives. Creating a licensing system for DIY biology labs and mandating registration for biohackers using sensitive technologies would help regulate these practices. Additionally, expanding existing regulatory frameworks to encompass small-scale genetic modification projects ensures that biohacking aligns with safety standards and reduces the risk of transnational crime associated with unmonitored genetic manipulation.

Data privacy is a growing concern, especially with the rise of biohacking, which brings new challenges for the General Data Protection Regulation (GDPR). Biohackers often collect and share personal health data without proper oversight, raising serious ethical and security concerns. Strengthening GDPR enforcement in biohacking communities - particularly with tailored guidelines for the collection of biometric and genetic data - is crucial. Ensuring that biohackers follow consent and data protection standards will help protect personal information and prevent its misuse for illegal purposes.

Creating ethical oversight through national committees for biohacking projects could also help manage the risks associated with data collection. It is vital for policymakers to collaborate with the biohacking community to address these issues effectively. By fostering open dialogue through workshops and advisory committees, regulators can gain a better understanding of biohacking while helping innovators navigate within clear legal frameworks. A regulatory sandbox could also offer a space for experimentation without the usual barriers, reducing the risk of enabling transnational crime. Building trust will be important, as some biohackers may see government involvement as a threat to their freedom to innovate.

An additional concern is liability and accountability in biohacking, especially in relation to transnational crime. The decentralized nature of biohacking makes it hard to pinpoint who is responsible when things go wrong - particularly with genetically modified organisms (GMOs) or failed self-experiments that could pose risks across borders. Developing clear liability frameworks would help establish who is accountable for damages from biohacking activities. Requiring biohackers to have liability insurance for high-risk endeavors could help mitigate potential harms. However, enforcement and identifying those responsible could be challenging, especially when many biohackers operate anonymously.

Policymakers must consider how unregulated biohacking can lead to exploitation, health risks, and ethical violations that span national borders. This calls for a comprehensive and adaptable legal framework that supports innovation while protecting against criminal misuse.

To foster a productive balance between innovation and safety, policymakers should focus on creating flexible, supportive frameworks that encourage responsible biohacking without stifling creativity or experimentation.

Rather than imposing overly strict regulations, the international community should adopt a more collaborative approach, working with the biohacking community to co-create guidelines that prioritize safety while respecting the autonomy of biohackers. This can be achieved by establishing a regulatory sandbox, where biohackers are given the freedom to innovate in a controlled and monitored environment. Such a framework would allow biohackers to experiment with cutting-edge technologies while receiving guidance on regulatory compliance and safety standards, ensuring that their work aligns with public health and ethical norms. At the same time, ensuring clearer liability guidelines for biohacking projects is important to protect both individuals and the public. Rather than imposing rigid enforcement, the focus should be on developing systems that provide clarity around accountability, while offering biohackers the flexibility to experiment safely. Closing the regulatory gaps in biohacking requires a balanced approach that promotes freedom and innovation while ensuring safety and ethical responsibility. Only in this manner can an environment be fostered that allows biohackers to continue pushing boundaries without being pushed into legal gray areas, thereby making a positive contribution to the future of biotechnology.

5.5. Data Protection and Crimes against Digital Economy

Data has emerged as a crucial asset that fuels the global economy, driving sectors ranging from artificial intelligence to e-commerce. This crucial resource has transformed economics, governance, and daily life, but it comes at a cost: the extensive collection, processing, and commodification of personal data raise significant concerns regarding privacy and individual rights. As corporations and governments accumulate vast troves of information, the potential for exploitation by criminal organizations increases, particularly in transnational crime. Criminal enterprises can leverage personal data for identity theft, fraud, fake news, terrorism, trafficking in human beings, blackmailing and other illicit activities that transcend borders, posing profound challenges to law enforcement agencies globally.

The growing commercialization and misuse of personal data raise urgent concerns about how to safeguard individuals within this rapidly evolving digital landscape. High-profile data breaches and cyberattacks have exposed vulnerabilities in modern data management techniques, revealing how sensitive information can be accessed, utilized, or manipulated by criminal actors. The anonymity afforded by the internet facilitates criminals' activities.

In response to these challenges, the EU introduced the GDPR in May 2018, establishing a robust legal framework aimed at regulating data usage and treating privacy as a fundamental right. This Regulation seeks to set a global benchmark for data governance, empowering individuals with greater control over their personal information and offering a layer of protection against misuse for criminal purposes.

The impacts of GDPR extend beyond Europe, inspiring regions such as ASEAN[61] and Latin America to develop their own data protection laws, recognizing the dual need for economic growth and privacy safeguards. The interplay between data protection and transnational crime is essential to examine, revealing not only the necessity for robust frameworks but also the vulnerabilities that emerge in our increasingly globalized digital economy. Within this context, it is evident that while data brings unprecedented opportunity, it simultaneously creates new avenues for crime that necessitate a coordinated international response.

Since its implementation, GDPR has redefined data privacy regulations, influencing not just Europe but the global stage. Its extraterritorial reach mandates compliance for organizations processing the data of EU citizens, regardless of their jurisdiction. This recognition that data protection must address international realities compels businesses and governments worldwide to adopt stringent data protection practices essential for mitigating the risks posed by transnational crime.

One significant aspect of GDPR is its potential deterrent effect on criminal enterprises. By establishing clear expectations for data protection and imposing severe penalties for non-compliance, GDPR increases the barriers for criminal actors seeking to exploit lax data protection frameworks.

Failure to comply with GDPR can result in hefty fines and legal repercussions, thus increasing the costs and risks associated with engaging in illicit activities. Criminal enterprises may reconsider using personal data for malicious purposes in jurisdictions with strict regulations like GDPR.

The recognition that transnational crime frequently exploits weak links in data protection mandates stronger cooperation among nations. Criminal enterprises often operate across jurisdictions, targeting those areas with lax data protection frameworks. This situation leads to the necessity for law enforcement and regulatory agencies to collaborate internationally, sharing

[61] M. K. Ariadno and A. H. Bajrektarevic, "Twinning Europe and Asia in Cyberspace: The EU Legislation ASEAN and Its Transformative Power," *Vision & Global Trends – International Institute for Global Analyzed* (2019).

information and strategies to combat the risks posed by cybercriminals. GDPR facilitates this international conversation by setting a standard that many countries aspire to meet, thereby enhancing collaborative efforts in fighting transnational crime.

Countries outside the EU are taking action to align their data protection laws with GDPR to facilitate international commerce[62] while safeguarding their citizens' data. For instance, Japan's adherence to GDPR principles exemplifies how nations can create meaningful partnerships while acknowledging the importance of protecting personal data[63]. Japan's move towards compliance has improved its economic standing by enabling smoother data transactions with European partners.

Furthermore, Latin American nations are also taking significant steps to bolster their data protection frameworks. Countries like Brazil, Mexico, Argentina, Colombia, and Ecuador are revising their legal systems to combat the misuse of personal data by criminal organizations. For example, Brazil's Lei Geral de Proteção de Dados[64] (LGPD), which closely mirrors GDPR, establishes stringent guidelines for how personal data should be handled, thereby placing accountability on organizations inevitably engaging in potentially exploitative practices.

5.5.1. The Broader Implications for Data Protection and Transnational Crime

The advent of GDPR and its adoption in regions like Latin America and the Caribbean[65] signify a proactive stance against transnational crime linked to data exploitation. The rise of the digital economy has prompted these nations to realize that inadequate data protection laws can create favorable environments for organized crime syndicates. These criminal networks are becoming increasingly adept at utilizing technology to access sensitive information, making it imperative for countries to strengthen their data protection frameworks.

---

[62] C. J. Hoofnagle, B. van der Sloot, and F. Zuiderveen Borgesius, "The European Union General Data Protection Regulation: What It Is and What It Means," *Information & Communications Technology Law* 28, no. 1 (2019): 65–98.

[63] Graham Greenleaf, "Global Data Privacy Laws 2019: 132 National Laws and Many Bills," *Privacy Laws & Business International Report* 157 (2019): 1–16.

[64] M. Marini and R. Figuereido, "Brazil's General Data Protection Law (LGPD): What You Need to Know," *Privacy International* (2019).

[65] Ibid.

Establishing robust data protection authorities (DPAs) in these regions is critical for enforcing compliance and fostering cooperation with international law enforcement agencies. DPAs are pivotal in not only regulating data protection practices but also in facilitating information sharing among countries to combat transnational crime. For instance, Brazil's Autoridade Nacional de Proteção de Dados (ANPD) plays an important role in ensuring compliance with LGPD while simultaneously addressing illicit activities such as data breaches and cyber fraud that operate internationally[66].

Moreover, strong data protection regulations facilitate international collaboration in addressing transnational crime. When countries implement GDPR-like laws, it supports a unified approach to data protection that can help identify and combat criminal tactics employed across borders. For example, joint task forces can leverage consistent data protection standards to track down cybercriminals involved in identity theft or human trafficking, promoting the sharing of critical intelligence and coordinated responses to compromised data.

Stricter data protection laws also highlight the need for businesses to adopt a culture of compliance that incorporates risk management strategies against data misuse. Organizations must be proactive in understanding how their data practices can contribute to or mitigate risks associated with transnational crime. This encompasses conducting regular audits, implementing robust cybersecurity measures, and educating employees about data protection practices. Such initiatives are essential not only for regulatory compliance but also for fostering a safe digital space that is less attractive to criminal activities.

In conjunction with enhancing individual data rights, the commitment to robust data protection plays is central to rebuilding public trust in digital systems. As citizens become increasingly aware of their rights and the risks associated with data exploitation, they can actively participate in safeguarding their information, which ultimately contributes to a broader societal effort to combat transnational crime. Herein lies the dual benefit of a comprehensive data protection regime: protecting individual privacy rights while fortifying the defenses against the threats posed by organized crime.

---

[66] M. Marini and R. Figuereido, "Brazil's General Data Protection Law."

5.5.2. Education and Awareness in the Context of Data Protection and Transnational Crime

As data protection laws continue to evolve, one thing is becoming increasingly clear: public awareness is just as important as regulation, especially when it comes to fighting transnational crime. People need to understand not only their rights when it comes to personal data, but also the risks they face when sharing it - and how to protect themselves. An informed public can act as a crucial first line of defense, making it harder for criminal networks to take advantage of vulnerabilities.

To achieve this, governments, civil society, and the private sector must work together to create strong public education campaigns. These should go beyond general messaging and address specific threats like identity theft, phishing, and cyber extortion. Public education should include the mechanics of these crimes, their indicators, and preventive strategies. Introducing digital literacy and cybersecurity awareness in schools, for example, would be a great way to start building these habits early on.

Businesses also have a big role to play. By being transparent about how they handle customer data, clearly explaining their privacy policies, and showing what steps they take to protect users, companies can help build a culture of trust and awareness. Beyond compliance, transparency fosters public trust in digital system.

Rights such data portability and the right to be forgotten are more than legal tools. They give individuals real control over their digital lives. And in doing so, they help protect not just privacy, but dignity - making sure no one is unfairly exposed, tracked, or exploited.

Raising awareness, promoting transparency, and empowering people to protect themselves is key to building resilience in the face of growing transnational cyber threats. Effective prevention begins with public awareness and digital literacy[67].

Collaboration between governmental agencies and private companies is also essential in enhancing cybersecurity infrastructure. By sharing best practices and establishing clear guidelines for data protection, businesses can contribute to a more secure digital environment, making it increasingly difficult for transnational criminals to exploit vulnerabilities.

---

[67] B. Zimmerman, "The Right to Be Forgotten and Its Implications for Social Media," *Journal of Law and Cyber Warfare* 8, no. 1 (2020): 50–68.

Besides educating individuals, countries should also invest in training police and other authorities to better understand transnational crimes related to data misuse. Specialized training programs can equip officers with the skills necessary to investigate and prevent cybercrime effectively. This approach is vital in ensuring that law enforcement agencies are prepared to deal with the sophisticated tactics employed by organized crime groups that operate on a global scale.

As the digital world evolves, so too must the technologies we use to protect personal data. Cryptography, for instance, has become essential for securing communication channels and preventing unauthorized access to sensitive information. By encrypting data both when it is stored and when it is being sent, organizations can reduce the risk of breaches and leaks, which are often exploited by criminals.

Emerging technologies, like artificial intelligence (AI), offer even greater potential to boost data protection. AI can quickly analyze large volumes of data, detecting unusual patterns that could signal a breach or fraudulent activity. This allows organizations to spot threats earlier, giving them a chance to act before any serious harm is done.

Blockchain offers a decentralized, tamper-resistant system that strengthens data integrity and auditability. Its decentralized design makes it resistant to tampering, ensuring that once information is recorded, it stays intact. This may enhance the security and integrity of personal data, reducing its appeal for criminal exploitation. At the same time, governments need to ensure their data protection laws keep up with technological advancements. These regulations can't be static - they need to evolve alongside new threats and tools. By regularly reviewing laws and engaging with experts from different sectors, governments can ensure that both national and international standards stay effective in combatting the sophisticated tactics criminals use today.

But while these technologies are crucial, they can't replace the need for human oversight and ethical considerations. As new tools emerge, we need clear ethical guidelines to ensure they are used responsibly. Data protection efforts must respect individual rights and ensure that new technologies do not create new vulnerabilities.

The fight against transnational crime related to data misuse must involve coordinated international efforts. Criminal organizations often exploit the differences in data protection laws across countries to their advantage, operating in areas where regulations are weak or inadequately enforced. Therefore, fostering international collaboration is essential for combating transnational crime effectively, ensuring that personal data is protected consistently across borders.

International treaties and agreements, such as the United Nations Conventions against Cybercrime and Budapest Convention on Cybercrime, provide frameworks for cooperation among nations in the realm of cybercrime. Such agreements facilitate mutual legal assistance and establish common standards for prosecuting cybercriminals, thereby enhancing the effectiveness of law enforcement efforts globally. Countries must be willing to engage in such partnerships, sharing information and resources to dismantle transnational criminal

Conclusion

Transnational crime undermines fundamental social frameworks and democratic institutions, and it has the capacity to destabilize governments and disrupt social order. Globalization brings great benefits but also presents complex challenges that extend beyond national borders. One of the key challenges is the complexity of transnational crime, which is expanding in a world of deepening global interdependence. A critical concern is the ability of transnational criminal organizations to function with relative impunity in regions where governance and law enforcement are weak or compromised. This obstructs effective prosecution and undermines state sovereignty, threatening the very essence of the rule of law.

The progression of transnational crime is starkly evident, as persistent threats such as drug trafficking or corruption continue alongside newly emerging forms of criminal activity. Criminal phenomena such as human trafficking, migrant smuggling, and terrorism financing take advantage of increased globalization. The widespread availability of small arms poses additional destabilizing effects on state security, particularly acute in regions such as the Americas and Africa. Drug trafficking not only endangers the well-being of citizens, and leads to a high level of criminality, but also poses a direct threat to state authorities, as organized crime networks occasionally challenge governmental control.

Central to these operations are issues of corruption, which serve as a fundamental threat to the heart of democracies. Corruption undermines governmental structures, depletes public resources, and erodes trust in leadership. By eroding institutional integrity, corruption facilitates a fertile ground for illicit activities and exacerbates the challenges states face to combating such crimes. The digital era, in particular, has accelerated the proliferation of new forms of crime. Criminal entities now exploit digital platforms that target individuals, corporations, and critical infrastructure, jeopardizing global security and stability. The rise of cryptocurrencies has injected further complexity into anti-money laundering frameworks, intensifying the call for comprehensive international regulatory mechanisms to oversee digital financial transactions.

Transnational crime syndicates have adeptly adopted new technologies, crafting sophisticated networks that pose severe legal challenges while menacing citizen rights and democratic integrity. These organizations infiltrate legitimate economic and political spheres, amplifying their corrosive effect and fostering systemic corruption, eroding public trust in essential institutions.

This chapter highlights the real and heightened risks posed by globalization, without adopting an alarmist tone. In light of these complex threats, an ambitious and collaborative international response is essential to safeguard democratic values, strengthen security frameworks, and uphold the rule of law across national boundaries.

The United Nations Convention against Transnational Organized Crime represented a key moment in international cooperation against organized crime. For the first time, nearly all countries around the world united in recognizing the pressing need to address transnational organized crime, a recognition made in the context of modern societal challenges. This international accord resulted in critical agreements that constituted a significant jump forward in the global criminal justice landscape.

In an era marked by polarization and conflict, it is not easy to imagine that nearly all states came together two decades ago to endorse innovative and ambitious anti-crime measures. Despite initial reluctance and arduous negotiations, the Palermo Convention - hailed by Kofi Annan as "the Millennium Summit" - was ultimately adopted, along with its three complementary protocols.

The Convention provides important tools for addressing corruption and money laundering within the broader fight against organized crime. It provided clear definitions of organized crime and introduced corporate liability, emphasizing the necessity of measures against money laundering and the confiscation of criminal proceeds. Furthermore, it laid out extensive victim protection protocols and concrete strategies for international cooperation, equipping member states with mechanisms to seek judicial assistance globally. Central authorities were envisioned to manage requests for cooperation while essential strategies in the international arena - such as joint investigative teams, the transfer of sentenced persons, and mutual legal assistance - were implemented. The UNTOC obligates member states to offer extensive cooperation, reinforcing the rule of law across borders.

Beyond cooperative measures, the UNTOC ambitiously extended victim protections, mandating restitution and protective measures. On the corporate front, it requires establishing civil, administrative, or criminal liability for companies failing to prevent serious transnational crimes. In the context of increasing corporate influence, especially multinational corporations, their participation in combating crimes is crucial. Corporations must play an active role in investigating crimes by implementing robust compliance programs to prevent their use for criminal activities. If they fail to take appropriate and effective measures, they must be subject to civil, criminal, or administrative liability. The enforcement of penalties must be sufficiently severe to encourage businesses to adopt comprehensive compliance and crime prevention strategies. Corporations operate with societal consent; in return, they are responsible for actively participating in crime prevention. Different industries face unique vulnerabilities, making their roles in mitigating specific types of crime especially significant. For instance, banks are pivotal in combating money laundering, given their central role in financial transactions. Similarly, companies in the primary sector must focus on preventing labor exploitation, while those in the tertiary sector are tasked with addressing issues like sexual exploitation.

The responsibility is particularly salient for companies that operate online. Strategies should include proactive monitoring and reporting mechanisms aimed at identifying and mitigating risks associated with transnational organized crime and, for example, online companies must provide clear warnings about the use of their platforms for exploiting vulnerable individuals or, including those offering virtual private network (VPN) services should actively cooperate with law enforcement agencies to enhance security measures. Online companies should proactively raise user awareness about internet risks. Adult website companies must take measures to prevent cases of human trafficking, just as social media companies should work to prevent crimes from being committed through their platforms.

Companies must be held to higher standards regarding compliance, particularly in their commitment to preventing crimes associated with their operations. This compliance includes incorporating robust compliance plans that encompass ethical guidelines, employee training on recognizing signs of exploitation, and implementing technology-driven solutions to enhance detection and reporting processes. Such initiatives safeguard vulnerable populations and reinforce the integrity of the business by aligning corporate actions with societal values and legal obligations.

In summary, corporations benefit from the societal framework that enables their operations and they must embrace their responsibility to contribute actively to crime prevention efforts. By doing so, they can play a crucial role in creating a safer, more responsible environment that discourages criminal activities and protects at-risk individuals within a society.

The legacy of the Palermo Convention lies in uniting countries around a shared acknowledgement of transnational crime and in its ambitious, groundbreaking measures. The Convention presents a robust model for combating transnational organized crime networks by fostering international collaboration. Corporate accountability, victim protection, and asset confiscation offer a comprehensive framework for authorities to tackle contemporary criminal challenges.

Despite these achievements, efficient international cooperation relies fundamentally on mutual respect and trust among states. In the current climate of prevalent conflicts, criminal organizations exploit weaknesses in international cooperation to evade justice and protect their assets. Therefore, maintaining and enhancing these cooperative frameworks remains a critical task. The collaborative spirit and innovative measures introduced by the Palermo Convention serve as a powerful reminder of what can be achieved through unified international efforts against the ever-evolving landscape of transnational crime.

The impact of the UNTOC was significantly enhanced through the incorporation of the three Protocols, which broadened its regulatory scope. The Protocols specifically addressed the trafficking of human beings, the smuggling of migrants, and arms trafficking, effectively filling a critical regulatory gap in international law that previously left these serious offenses, in many cases, unregulated. In contrast, more widely regulated crimes such as drug trafficking and terrorism; these transnational crimes were mainly unaddressed by international norms and suffered from a minimal cooperative engagement due to their absence from the domestic legislation of numerous nations.

These Protocols played a key role in tackling serious transnational crimes that had previously lacked coordinated international regulation. By strategically opting to focus on transnational crime as a broader category rather than isolated offenses, the UNTOC positioned to respond effectively to emerging criminal patterns fueled by technological advancements and globalization.

The Protocols of the UNTOC offered concrete solutions to crimes and phenomena under-recognized worldwide by States, proving to be effective mechanisms in the fight against specific criminal activities. The need to combat modern-day slavery has been widely acknowledged mainly thanks to the Palermo Protocol against Trafficking in Human Beings, emphasizing the importance of international cooperation and the integration of anti-human trafficking measures into domestic laws. The Protocols also clarified distinctions between human trafficking and migrant smuggling, often conflated, and have served as the groundwork for more advanced regulatory frameworks 20 years later. Human trafficking is one of the most pressing scourges of our time. Despite the formal abolition of slavery, current data suggests there are more individuals enslaved today than at any previous point in history, exacerbated by globalization and the vulnerability and poverty of victims. On the other hand, the smuggling of migrants presents a significant challenge for states today, underscoring the urgent need to address migration bravely and decisively. This is particularly urgent because many migrants rely on smuggling networks placing them in severe danger and thousands of migrants perish as traffickers' priorities profit over safety. Although the Protocol against the Illicit Manufacturing of and Trafficking in Firearms has seen less widespread acceptance, it addresses one of the most significant issues related to violence and destabilization: the prevalence of small arms. Raising awareness and encouraging states to adopt the Firearms Protocol remains a key priority. Transnational criminal organizations are increasingly powerful, exploiting globalization and advancing technologies to expand their reach and influence.

The UNTOC plays a key role as a complementary framework to the existing legal instruments and conventions to combat serious offenses. It, for example, complements specialized legal instruments such as the United Nations Convention against Corruption and various treaties addressing drug-related crimes and terrorism. The UNTOC represents a fundamental tool for enhancing international cooperation in the fight against transnational crime, focusing on shared responsibilities and collective action among states. The UNTOC facilitates the exchange of information, intelligence, and resources necessary to dismantle complex criminal networks transcending borders by uniting nations under a common legal framework.

Given the sophistication of modern transnational crime, this collaborative approach is crucial, as it often leverages technological advancements to evade law enforcement, launder money, and expand operations.

The specialized conventions provide targeted solutions, enabling member states to tackle the unique challenges posed by each specific offence. The UNCAC, for instance, focuses on enhancing the integrity of public and private sectors, fostering transparency, and holding individuals accountable. In parallel, drug trafficking conventions establish comprehensive frameworks for investigating and prosecuting drug-related offenses, highlighting the intricate relationship between drug cartels and organized crime.

As transnational organized crime continues to evolve, legislative measures must reflect the changing dynamics of illicit activities. The interaction between the UNTOC and related legal frameworks reflects a unified approach to addressing the global, multifaceted nature of transnational crime. For instance, the UNTOC can facilitate the effective implementation of strategies against corruption, which often serves as a facilitator for both drug trafficking and terrorism. By addressing the root causes of these crimes through cohesive legal measures, states can enhance their capacity to combat them effectively.

The significance of the UNTOC is further magnified in the face of the modern challenges of globalization and technological advancements. Criminal organizations are skilled at exploiting existing vulnerabilities and creating new avenues for their operations. The rise of the Internet and digital finance has given criminals unprecedented opportunities, leading to a surge in cybercrime and innovative schemes that can evade traditional law enforcement tactics. Therefore, the UNTOC's adaptability is crucial; it provides a foundational framework that can evolve with shifting criminal methodologies, ensuring that states are equipped to respond to both traditional and emerging threats.

Ultimately, the persistence of classic transnational crimes amidst the rise of new illicit activities reinforce the critical importance of adopting a multifaceted and agile approach. By utilizing the UNTOC alongside complementary international agreements, nations can enhance their efforts to confront the evolving nature of transnational crime while also addressing the underlying issues that facilitate these offenses. The collective endeavor to combat these challenges not only protects vulnerable populations from exploitation and violence but also contributes to the maintenance of democratic principles and societal integrity in an increasingly complex world. As nations work together, leveraging the synergies created by the UNTOC, its Protocols, and other international conventions that address specific international crimes, the international community can foster a safer, more responsible environment - one that can withstand the sophisticated tactics used by transnational criminal organizations.

The UNTOC should be regarded as a dynamic instrument that can adapt to evolving forms of organized crime. The framework's efficacy does not lie solely in its mechanisms but rather in the commitment of nations to utilize these established tools to confront transnational organized crime effectively. The UNTOC lays the groundwork for the fight against organized crime, emphasizing international cooperation, corporate responsibility, and the recovery of proceeds from criminal activities.

However, the real challenge resides in the global awareness and legislative framework surrounding these issues. Many states still lack domestic laws to address emerging crimes, such as environmental offenses or data protection issues, which are becoming increasingly relevant in our technologically advanced world. The experience gained from the Palermo Protocols illustrates that, despite seeming impossible, states can transcend barriers and reservations to combat transnational crime collaboratively. These challenges affect all nations without exception, and the interconnected nature of global crime necessitates a united front.

However, the current geopolitical divisions complicate international efforts to combat organized crime. Criminal organizations are well-positioned to exploit these divisions in order to expand their influence and consolidate power. Therefore, we must recognize the potential for unprecedented destructive challenges on the horizon. Hence, there can be no justification for states to fail to reach a consensus on addressing emerging threats. The advent of the internet and artificial intelligence represents a revolutionary shift with profound implications for the nature of crime. While these advancements offer numerous benefits to society, they simultaneously provide new avenues for criminal exploitation that could far exceed the capabilities of traditional crimes. The urgency for states to collaborate effectively, share information, and develop robust legal frameworks that encompass these new realities cannot be overstated.

There must be international pressure to ensure that no state underestimates the risks presented by new challenges, as each country is susceptible to these threats. No state is immune to crimes committed via the Internet, and the challenges related to cybersecurity, privacy, and environmental offenses pose complex questions regarding their magnitude and impact. We currently face the proliferation of new crimes that can affect us all, such as cyber fraud, trafficking in counterfeit medications, identity theft, or phishing schemes. Other potential criminal activities we have yet to encounter, such as spreading fake news and other digital crimes, could jeopardize social cohesion.

Given the severity and complexity of these emerging threats, international cooperation is not merely desirable - it is imperative. There can be no justification for states delaying or avoiding collaborative efforts to address these challenges. The mechanisms established through the UNTOC Protocols are crucial, as are international conventions that provide a legal framework for addressing transnational crime effectively. Under the auspices of the United Nations, these legal instruments serve multiple purposes: they raise awareness of these challenges, facilitate the harmonization of national legislation, and promote international cooperation in the fight against crime.

In this context, fostering international collaboration is essential. Governments must share information, resources, and best practices to counter these evolving threats effectively.

By working together and committing to a united front against such crimes, we can enhance our resilience to the ever-changing landscape of criminality. The collective will to confront these challenges must be evident, ensuring that we leverage existing frameworks to foster comprehensive responses. Ultimately, the fight against transnational crime requires unwavering commitment, awareness, and cooperation on a global scale to protect our societies and maintain democratic values in an increasingly complex world.

In a world where transnational crime continues to evolve and undermine the foundations of democracy and social order, a collective commitment to international cooperation, strong legal frameworks, and proactive engagement is not only essential—it is essential to safeguard the rights, dignity, and security of individuals worldwide.

References

Airapetean, Artur, and Andreea Corsei. "International Legal Framework on Human Trafficking." *Acta Universitatis Danubius* 18, no. 3 (2022).

Alarcón Jiménez, Oscar, María Elósegui Itxaso, Carmen Morte Gómez, Anna Maria Mengual, and Guillem Cano. *Construyendo los Derechos Humanos en Estrasburgo: el Tribunal Europeo de Derechos Humanos y el Consejo de Europa*. Valencia: Tirant Lo Blanch, (2020).

Aljehani, A. "The Legal Definition of the Smuggling of Migrants in Light of the Provisions of the Migrant Smuggling Protocol." *The Journal of Criminal Law* 79, no. 2 (2015): 130–131.

Ariadno, M. K., and A. H. Bajrektarevic. "Twinning Europe and Asia in Cyberspace : The EU Legislation ASEAN and Its Transformative Power." *Vision & Global Trends – International Institute for Global Analyses* (2019).

Bajrektarevic, A., and D. Karantzeni. *Cybersecurity : Essentials – Institutions, Instruments, Types and Forms*. New York : NOVA Science Publishers, (2015).

Balsamo, Antonio. "Twenty Years Later: The New Perspectives of the Palermo Convention." *Dibattito* 6, no. 3 (2020): 11.

Battleday, R. M., and A.-K. Brem. "Modafinil for Cognitive Neuroenhancement in Healthy Non-Sleep-Deprived Subjects: A Systematic Review." *European Neuropsychopharmacology* 25, no. 11 (2015): 1865–1881.

Betti, Stefano. "New Prospects for Interstate Cooperation in Criminal Matters: The Palermo Convention." *International Criminal Law Review* (2003): 172.

Binder, J. F., and J. Kenyon. "Terrorism and the Internet: How Dangerous Is Online Radicalization?" *Frontiers in Psychology* 13 (October 13, 2022).

Brickey, Kathleen F. "Corporate Criminal Accountability: A Brief History and Observation." *Washington University Law Quarterly* 60 (1982): 393–397.

Brodowski, Dominik, Manuel Espinoza de los Monteros de la Parra, and Klaus Tiedemann. *Regulating Corporate Criminal Liability: An Introduction*. Cham: Springer International Publishing, (2014).

Campana, Paolo, and Federico Varese. "Exploitation in Human Trafficking and Smuggling." *European Journal of Crime Policy and Research* 22 (2016): 89–105.

Coenen, Christopher. "Biohacking: New Do-It-Yourself Practices as Technoscientific Work between Freedom and Necessity." *Proceedings* 1, no. 3 (2017): 256.

Coventry, Thea. "Seizing Stateless Smuggling Vessels on the Mediterranean High Seas." *Leiden Journal of International Law* 36, no. 4 (2023): 946–950.

Csontos-Nagy, Ivett. "International Criminal Cooperation in the Shadow of the Coronavirus Pandemic." *AARMS* 22, no. 1 (2023): 35.

Delfanti, Alessandro. *Biohackers: The Politics of Open Science*. Cambridge: Polity, (2013).

European Commission, Directorate-General for Migration and Home Affairs. *Call to Action on a Global Alliance to Counter Migrant Smuggling*. Luxembourg: Publications Office of the European Union, (November 28, 2023)

Fuisz, Richard. "Caveat Creator." *Journal of Law and the Biosciences* 4, no. 3 (December 2017): 658–670.

Gardiner, Alan H., and S. Langdon. "The Treaty of Alliance Between Ḫattušili, King of the Hittites, and the Pharaoh Ramesses II of Egypt." *The Journal of Egyptian Archaeology* 6, no. 3 (July 1920): 179–205.

Greenleaf, Graham. "Global Data Privacy Laws 2019: 132 National Laws and Many Bills." *Privacy Laws & Business International Report* 157 (2019): 1–16.

Hideg, Gergely, and Anna Alvazzi del Frate. *Still Not There: Global Violent Deaths Scenarios, 2019–2030*. Small Arms Survey Briefing Paper, (February 2021).

Hillion, Christophe. "Enlarging the European Union and Deepening Its Fundamental Rights Protection." *Swedish Institute for European Policy Studies* (June 2013): 2.

Hoofnagle, C. J., B. van der Sloot, and F. Zuiderveen Borgesius. "The European Union General Data Protection Regulation: What It Is and What It Means." *Information & Communications Technology Law* 28, no. 1 (2019): 65–98.

International Centre for Migration Policy Development. *The Relationship Between Organised Crime and Trafficking in Aliens*. Vienna: ICMPD, (2010).

International Organization for Migration (IOM). World Migration Report. Geneva, (June 2022).

Kadir, Nadiah Khaeriah, Judhariksawan, and Maskun. "Terrorism and Cyberspace: A Phenomenon of Cyber-Terrorism as Transnational Crimes." *Fiat Justisia* 13, no. 4 (2020): 335.

Kahathuduwa, Chanaka N., Tharaka L. Dassanayake, A. M. Tissa Amarakoon, and Vajira S. Weerasinghe. "Acute Effects of Theanine, Caffeine and Theanine–Caffeine Combination on Attention." *Nutritional Neuroscience* 20, no. 6 (2016): 369–377

Karp, Aaron. *Estimating Global Civilian-Held Firearms Numbers*. Geneva: Small Arms Survey, (June 2018).

Kelly, R. J. "Introduction: Organized Crime Penetrations of Legitimate Businesses." In *The Upperworld and the Underworld: Criminal Justice and Public Safety*, edited by R. J. Kelly. Boston, MA: Springer, (1999).

Luyten, Katrien, and Sofija Voronova. "Understanding the EU Response to Organised Crime." *European Parliamentary Research Service*, (September 2009).

McCarthy-Jones, Anthea, Caroline Doyle, and Mark Turner. "From Hierarchies to Networks: The Organizational Evolution of the International Drug Trade." *International Journal of Law, Crime and Justice* (August 2020).

Meyer, M. "Biohacking." In *The Handbook of Peer Production*, edited by M. O'Neil, C. Pentzold, and S. Toupin, 211–224. Malden, MA: Wiley-Blackwell, (2020).

National Institute of Standards and Technology. Artificial Intelligence Risk Management Framework. Gaithersburg, MD: U.S. Department of Commerce, (January 2023).

Office to Monitor and Combat Trafficking in Persons. *Human Trafficking and Migrant Smuggling: Understanding the Difference*. Washington, DC: U.S. Department of State, (June 2017).

Organisation for Economic Co-operation and Development. *Liability of Legal Persons for Corruption in Eastern Europe and Central Asia*. Paris: OECD Publishing, (2015).

Organization for Security and Co-operation in Europe (OSCE). *Handbook of Best Practices on Small Arms and Light Weapons*. Vienna, (2003).

Schloenhardt, Andreas, and Hadley Macdonald. "Barriers to Ratification of the United Nations Protocol Against the Smuggling of Migrants." *Asian Journal of International Law* 7, no. 1 (2017): 13–38.

Schloenhardt, Andreas, and J. E. Dale. "Twelve Years On: Revisiting the UN Protocol Against the Smuggling of Migrants by Land, Sea and Air." *Zeitschrift für Öffentliches Recht* 67 (2012): 129–156.

Sherman, John. *Beyond CSR: The Story of the UN Guiding Principles on Business and Human Rights*. Cambridge, MA: Harvard Kennedy School, (March 2020).

Siller, Nicole J. "Human Trafficking in International Law Before the Palermo Protocol." *Netherlands International Law Review* (2017): 2.

Soriano, Juan Pablo. "Gobernanza Global Contra la Delincuencia Transnacional: La UE y la Convención de Palermo." *Revista CIDOB d'Afers Internacionals*, no. 108 (2015): 142.

Tennant, Ian. "Fulfilling the Promise of Palermo? A Political History of the UN Convention Against Transnational Organized Crime." *Journal of Illicit Economies and Development* 2, no. 1 (2020): 53.

United Nations Office of the High Commissioner for Human Rights, United Nations High Commissioner for Refugees, United Nations Children's Fund (UNICEF), United Nations Office on Drugs and Crime, UN Women, and International Labour Organization . *Joint UN Commentary on the EU Directive: A Human Rights Based Approach*. (2011).

United Nations Office of the High Commissioner for Human Rights. *Guiding Principles on Business and Human Rights: Implementing the United Nations "Protect, Respect and Remedy" Framework*. New York and Geneva: United Nations, (2011).

United Nations Office on Drugs and Crime. *A Century of International Drug Control*. Vienna, (2008).

United Nations Office on Drugs and Crime. *Drug Trafficking as a Security Threat in West Africa. Vienna(2008).*

United Nations Office on Drugs and Crime. *Technical Guide to the Implementation of the Protocol Against the Illicit Manufacturing of and Trafficking in Firearms*. New York: United Nations, (2011).

Valverde Cano, Ana B. "Reexaminando la Definición de Trata de Seres Humanos del Protocolo de Palermo: La Trata como Forma de Explotación." *Estudios de Deusto* 67, no. 2 (2019): 11–12.

Van Dijk, Jan J. M. "Empowering Victims of Organized Crime: On the Concurrence of the Palermo Convention with the UN Declaration on Basic Principles of Justice for Victims." *International Review of Victimology* 9 (2002): 23.

Watson, Hope. "Pornography-Based Sex Trafficking: A Palermo Protocol Fit for the Internet Age." *Vanderbilt Law Review* 54 (2021): 495-520.

Treaties and International Instruments

African Union. African Union Convention for the Protection and Assistance of Internally Displaced Persons in Africa. (October 23, 2009).

African Union. Convention on the Ban of the Import into Africa and the Control of Transboundary Movement and Management of Hazardous Wastes within Africa. Adopted by 51 African countries, Bamako, Mali, (January 30, 1991).

African Union. Heads of State and Government of the Member States of the Organization of African Unity. Constitutive Act of the African Union. (July 1, 2000).

African Union. Protocol to the OAU Convention on the Prevention and Combating of Terrorism. July 8, 2004.

Convention on Access to Information, Public Participation in Decision-Making and Access to Justice in Environmental Matters (June 25, 1998).

Council of Europe. Additional Protocol to the Council of Europe Convention on the Prevention of Terrorism. (May 19, 2015).

Council of Europe. Convention Against Trafficking in Human Organs, (March 25, 2015).

Council of Europe. Convention Established by the Council in Accordance with Article 34 of the Treaty on European Union, on Mutual Assistance in Criminal Matters Between the Member States of the European Union. Official Journal of the European Union L 197 (July 12, 2000).

Council of Europe. Convention for the Protection of Human Rights and Dignity of the Human Being with regard to the Application of Biology and Medicine: Convention on Human Rights and Biomedicine. (April 4, 1997)

Council of Europe. Convention on Artificial Intelligence and Human Rights, Democracy and the Rule of Law, (September 5, 2024).

Council of Europe. Convention on Cybercrime, (November 23, 2001).

Council of Europe. Convention on Intelligence and Human Rights, Democracy, and the Rule of Law, (May 17, 2024).

Council of Europe. Convention on Preventing and Combating Violence Against Women and Domestic Violence, (May 11, 2011).

Council of Europe. Convention on the Counterfeiting of Medical Products and Similar Crimes Involving Threats to Public Health, (October 28, 2011).

Council of Europe. Convention on the Prevention of Terrorism, (May 16, 2005).

Council of Europe. Council of Europe Convention on Action Against Trafficking in Human Beings, (May 16, 2005).

Council of Europe. European Convention on Mutual Assistance in Criminal Matters, 30 (April 20, 1959).

Council of Europe. European Convention on the Suppression of Terrorism, (January 27, 1977).

Council of Europe. Explanatory Report to the Convention on Cybercrime, (November 23, 2001).

Council of Europe. Framework Convention on Offences Relating to Cultural Property, (May 3, 2017).

Council of the European Union. Framework Decision 2006/783/JHA on the Principle of Mutual Recognition to Confiscation Orders (October 6, 2006).

European Union. Directive 2008/99/EC of the European Parliament and of the Council of November 19, 2008, on the Protection of the Environment through Criminal Law). OJ L 328 (December 6, 2008): 28–37.

European Union. Directive 98/44/EC of the European Parliament and of the Council of July 6, 1998, on the Legal Protection of Biotechnological Inventions.

European Union, Directive 2024/1712 on preventing and combating trafficking in human beings and protecting its victims, (June 13, 2024)

European Union, Regulation (EC) No. 1829/2003 on Genetically Modified Food and Feed. (September 22, 2003).

European Union, Regulation (EU) 2017/745 on Medical Devices. (April 5, 2017).

European Union. A European Agenda on Migration, Communication from the Commission, COM (May 13 , 2015)

European Union. Communication from the Commission on the EU Strategy to Tackle Organised Crime 2021–2025. April 14, 2021).

European Union. Consolidated Version of the Treaty on the Functioning of the European Union, 2008/C 115/01 (December 13, 2007).

European Union. Council Decision of 6 April 2009 Establishing the European Police Office (Europol). Official Journal of the European Union L 121 (May 15, 2009): 37–66

European Union. Council Regulation (EU) 2017/1939 of 12 October 2017 Implementing Enhanced Cooperation on the Establishment of the European Public Prosecutor's Office ('the EPPO'). Official Journal of the European Union L 283 (October 31, 2017): 1–71.

European Union. Directive (EU) 2024/1203 of the European Parliament and of the Council of April 11, 2024, on the Protection of the Environment through Criminal Law. OJ L 2024/1203 (April 30, 2024).

European Union. Directive 2001/18/EC of the European Parliament and of the Council of March 12, 2001, on the Deliberate Release into the Environment of Genetically Modified Organisms. (March 12, 2001)

European Union. Directive 2001/18/EC on the Deliberate Release into the Environment of Genetically Modified Organisms and Repealing Council Directive 90/220/EEC (March 12, 2001).

European Union. Directive 2005/35/EC of the European Parliament and of the Council of September 7, 2005, on Ship-Source Pollution and on the Introduction of Penalties for Infringements. OJ L 255 (September 30, 2005).

European Union. Directive 2014/41/EU of the European Parliament and of the Council of April 3, 2014, Regarding the European Investigation Order in Criminal Matters. Official Journal of the European Union L 130 (May 1, 2014).

European Union. Directive 2014/95/EU of the European Parliament and of the Council of October 22, 2014, Amending Directive 2013/34/EU as Regards Disclosure of Non-

Financial and Diversity Information by Certain Large Undertakings and Groups. OJ L 330 (November 15, 2014): 1–9.
European Union. Directive 2022/2464 of the European Parliament and of the Council of December 14, 2022, Amending Regulation No. 537/2014, Directive 2004/109/EC, Directive 2006/43/EC, and Directive 2013/34/EU, as Regards Corporate Sustainability Reporting. (December 14, 2022)
European Union. Regulation No. 1829/2003 of the European Parliament and of the Council of September 22, 2003, on Genetically Modified Food and Feed. (September 22, 2003)
European Union. Regulation (EU) 2016/679 of the European Parliament and of the Council of April 27, 2016, on the Protection of Natural Persons with Regard to the Processing of Personal Data and on the Free Movement of Such Data. (April 27, 2016)
European Union. Regulation. 2017/745 of the European Parliament and of the Council of April 5, 2017, on Medical Devices. (April 5, 2017)
European Union. Regulation. No. 536/2014 of the European Parliament and of the Council of April 16, 2014, on Clinical Trials on Medicinal Products for Human Use, and Repealing Directive 2001/20/EC.
European Union. Treaty of Lisbon Amending the Treaty on European Union and the Treaty Establishing the European Community (December 13, 2007).
European Union. Treaty on European Union (Consolidated Version), Treaty of Maastricht. Official Journal of the European Communities C 325/5 (February 7, 1992).
International Civil Aviation Organization. Convention for the Suppression of Unlawful Acts Against the Safety of Civil Aviation. 974 U.N.T.S. 177 (September 23, 1971).
International Civil Aviation Organization. Convention on International Civil Aviation. 15 U.N.T.S. 295 (December 7, 1944).
International Civil Aviation Organization. Protocol for the Suppression of Unlawful Acts of Violence at Airports Serving International Civil Aviation, supplementary to the Convention for the Suppression of Unlawful Acts Against the Safety of Civil Aviation. (February 24, 1988).
International Maritime Organization. Convention on the International Maritime Organization. entered into force March 17, 1958. (March 6, 1948).
Interpol. Organized Crime, Resolution No. AGN/57/RES/17, (November 23, 1988).
League of Arab States. Arab Convention on the Suppression of Terrorism (April 22, 1998).
League of Nations. Agreement Concerning the Suppression of the Manufacture of, Internal Trade in, and Use of, Prepared Opium. Geneva, February 11, 1925; and Protocol Amending the Agreements, Conventions, and Protocols on Narcotic Drugs, concluded at The Hague (1912), Geneva (1925, 1931).
League of Nations. Convention to Suppress the Slave Trade and Slavery, 60 LNTS 253, Registered No. 1414 (September 25, 1926).
League of Nations. International Opium Convention. The Hague, January 23, 1912.
Organization of African Unity Charter of the Organization of African Unity (May 25, 1963).
Organization of African Unity. Convention on the Prevention and Combating of Terrorism. (June 14, 1999).
Organization of African Unity. OAU Convention on the Prevention and Combating of Terrorism (June 14, 1999).

Organization of American States. Convention to Prevent and Punish the Acts of Terrorism Taking the Form of Crimes Against Persons and Related Extortion That Are of International Significance. OAS Treaty Series, No. 37 (February 2, 1971).

Organization of American States. Inter-American Convention Against Terrorism. (March 6, 2002).

Organization of American States. Inter-American Convention on Extradition (February 25, 1981).

Organization of American States. American Convention on Human Rights (November 22, 1969),

Organization of Islamic Cooperation. Convention of the Organization of the Islamic Conference on Combating International Terrorism, Annex to Resolution No. 59/26-P (July 1, 1999).

South Asian Association for Regional Cooperation (SAARC). Regional Convention on the Suppression of Terrorism (November 4, 1987).

South Asian Association for Regional Cooperation, Additional Protocol to the SAARC Regional Convention on Suppression of Terrorism (January 6, 2004).

United Kingdom of Great Britain and Northern Ireland, United States of America, France, and Union of Soviet Socialist Republics. Charter of the International Military Tribunal (London Agreement). (August 8, 1945).

United Nations Educational, Scientific and Cultural Organization. UNESCO Universal Declaration on Cultural Diversity. (November 2, 2001).

United Nations General Assembly. 1972 Protocol Amending the Single Convention on Narcotic Drugs, 1961, A/RES/3444 (December 9, 1972).

United Nations General Assembly. Convention on Offences and Certain Acts Committed on Board Aircraft. (September 14, 1963).

United Nations General Assembly. Convention on the Prevention and Punishment of Crimes Against Internationally Protected Persons, Including Diplomatic Agents, A/RES/3166 (December 14, 1973).

United Nations General Assembly. Declaration on Principles of International Law Concerning Friendly Relations and Cooperation Among States in Accordance with the Charter of the United Nations, A/RES/2625(XXV) (October 24, 1970).

United Nations General Assembly International Convention for the Suppression of the Financing of Terrorism, No. 38349 (December 9, 1999).

United Nations General Assembly. 1971 Convention on Psychotropic Substances, A/RES/3443 (December 9, 1975).

United Nations General Assembly. Arms Trade Treaty, Resolution 67/234B (April 2, 2013).

United Nations General Assembly. Constitution of the World Health Organization, A/RES/131 (November 17, 1948).

United Nations General Assembly. Convention for the Suppression of Unlawful Acts Against the Safety of Maritime Navigation, No. 29004 (March 10, 1988).

United Nations General Assembly. Convention for the Suppression of Unlawful Seizure of Aircraft. UN Treaty Series, (December 16, 1970).

United Nations General Assembly. Convention on the Elimination of All Forms of Discrimination Against Women. United Nations Treaty Series 1249 (December 18, 1979).

United Nations General Assembly. Convention on the Marking of Plastic Explosives for the Purpose of Detection (March 1, 1991).

United Nations General Assembly. Convention on the Physical Protection of Nuclear Material, No. 24631 (October 26, 1979).

United Nations General Assembly. Convention on the Rights of the Child. United Nations Treaty Series 1577 (November 20, 1989): 3.

United Nations General Assembly. Declaration of Basic Principles of Justice for Victims of Crime and Abuse of Power, A/RES/40/34 (November 29, 1985).

United Nations General Assembly. High-level Political Signing Conference for the United Nations Convention Against Transnational Organized Crime, A/RES/54/129 (January 28, 2000).

United Nations General Assembly. International Convention Against the Taking of Hostages, No. 21931 (November 17, 1979).

United Nations General Assembly. International Convention for the Suppression of Acts of Nuclear Terrorism, A/RES/59/290 (April 15, 2005).

United Nations General Assembly. International Convention for the Suppression of Terrorist Bombings, No. 37517 (December 15, 1997).

United Nations General Assembly. International Convention for the Suppression of the Financing of Terrorism, No. 38349 (December 9, 1999).

United Nations General Assembly. International Covenant on Civil and Political Rights. United Nations Treaty Series 999 (December 16, 1966): 171.

United Nations General Assembly. Minamata Convention on Mercury. (October 10, 2013).

United Nations General Assembly. Naples Political Declaration and Global Action Plan Against Organized Transnational Crime, A/RES/49/159 (February 24, 1995).

United Nations General Assembly. Protocol Against the Illicit Manufacturing of and Trafficking in Firearms, Their Parts and Components, and Ammunition, Supplementing the United Nations Convention Against Transnational Organized Crime, A/RES/55/255 (May 31, 2001).

United Nations General Assembly. Protocol Against the Smuggling of Migrants by Land, Sea and Air, Supplementing the United Nations Convention Against Transnational Organized Crime (New York, November 15, 2000). Entry into force January 28, 2004.

United Nations General Assembly. Protocol for the Suppression of Unlawful Acts Against the Safety of Fixed Platforms Located on the Continental Shelf. UNTS 1678, I-29004 (March 10, 1988).

United Nations General Assembly. Protocol to Prevent, Suppress and Punish Trafficking in Persons, Especially Women and Children, Supplementing the United Nations Convention Against Transnational Organized Crime (November 15, 2000).

United Nations General Assembly. Resolution 66/10: United Nations Counter-Terrorism Centre, A/RES/66/10 (December 7, 2011).

United Nations General Assembly. Resolution 71/291: Strengthening the Capability of the United Nations System to Assist Member States in Implementing the UN Global Counter-Terrorism Strategy, A/RES/71/291 (June 15, 2017).

United Nations General Assembly. Resolution A/RES/53/111 (January 20, 1999).

United Nations General Assembly. Rome Statute of the International Criminal Court, (July 17, 1998).

United Nations General Assembly. Single Convention on Narcotic Drugs (March 31,1961).

United Nations General Assembly. Convention on Psychotropic Substances (Ferbuary 21, 1971)

United Nations General Assembly. Convention against Illicit Traffic in Narcotic Drugs and Psychotropic Substances (December 20, 1988).

United Nations General Assembly. The Basel Convention on the Control of Transboundary Movements of Hazardous Wastes and Their Disposal, (March 22, 1989).

United Nations General Assembly. The United Nations Global Counter-Terrorism Strategy, A/RES/60/288 (September 20, 2006).

United Nations General Assembly. Transforming Our World: The 2030 Agenda for Sustainable Development, A/RES/70/1 (October 21, 2015).

United Nations General Assembly. United Nations Convention Against Transnational Organized Crime, A/RES/55/25 (January 8, 2001).

United Nations General Assembly. United Nations Convention Against Corruption, A/58/422 (October 31, 2003).

United Nations General Assembly. United Nations Convention Against Illicit Traffic in Narcotic Drugs and Psychotropic Substances. (December 19, 1988).

United Nations General Assembly. Vienna Declaration on Crime and Justice: Meeting the Challenges of the Twenty-First Century. 10th United Nations Congress on the Prevention of Crime and the Treatment of Offenders, (January 17, 2001)

United Nations General Assembly. Draft United Nations Convention Against Cybercrime: Strengthening International Cooperation for Combating Certain Crimes Committed by Means of Information and Communications Technology Systems. Hanoi, (December 24, 2024).

United Nations General Assembly. United Nations Convention on the Law of the Sea, (December 10, 1982).

United Nations Office on Drugs and Crime. Resolution 10/6: Preventing and Combating Crimes that Affect the Environment Falling within the Scope of the United Nations Convention against Transnational Organized Crime, (October 16, 2020).

United Nations Security Council Counter-Terrorism Committee. Delhi Declaration on Countering the Use of New and Emerging Technologies for Terrorist Purposes. New Delhi, (October 29, 2022).

United Nations Security Council. Resolution 1373 (2001): Threats to International Peace and Security Caused by Terrorist Acts, S/RES/1373 (September 28, 2001).

Online Resources

African Union. *Kampala Convention*, art. 9(1). Accessed September 29, 2024. https://au.int/sites/default/files/treaties/36846-treaty-kampala_convention.pdf.

Asian Development Bank. "Publications and Documents." Accessed November 29, 2024. https://www.adb.org/documents/series/office-anticorruption-and-integrity-annual-report.

Asian Development Bank. "Who We Are." Accessed December 4, 2024. https://www.adb.org/who-we-are.

Cambridge Dictionary. s.v. "biohacking." Accessed November 24, 2024. https://dictionary.cambridge.org/dictionary/english/biohacking.

Council of Europe. "Chart of Signatures and Ratifications of Treaty 30." Accessed November 11, 2024. https://www.coe.int/en/web/conventions/full-list?module=signatures-by-treaty&treatynum=030

Council of Europe. "European Committee on Crime Problems." Accessed November 14, 2024. https://www.coe.int/en/web/cdpc/home.

Council of Europe. "Treaty Office." Accessed November 14, 2024. https://www.coe.int/en/web/conventions.

Council of Europe. *Resolution (99) 5 Establishing the Group of States Against Corruption (GRECO)*. Adopted May 1, 1999.

Cybercrime Atlas. "Building a Shared Knowledge Base to Disrupt Cybercrime." Accessed November 30, 2024. https://initiatives.weforum.org/cybercrime-atlas/home.

ENACSO. *European NGO Alliance for Child Safety Online*. Accessed September 11, 2024. http://www.enacso.eu/.

European Commission. "Global Approach to Migration and Mobility." Accessed November 22, 2024. https://home-affairs.ec.europa.eu/networks/european-migration-network-emn/emn-asylum-and-migration-glossary/glossary/global-approach-migration-and-mobility-gamm_en.

European Commission. "Horizon Europe." Accessed December 16, 2024. https://research-and-innovation.ec.europa.eu/funding/funding-opportunities/funding-programmes-and-open-calls/horizon-europe_en.

European Commission. "Information on SIRENE Cooperation." Accessed November 24, 2024. https://home-affairs.ec.europa.eu/policies/schengen-borders-and-visa/schengen-information-system/sirene-cooperation_fr.

European Commission. "Managing Migration Better in All Aspects: A European Agenda on Migration." Accessed November 24, 2024. https://ec.europa.eu/commission/presscorner/detail/en/ip_15_4956.

European Commission. "Managing Migration Better in All Aspects: A European Agenda on Migration." Accessed November 24, 2024. https://ec.europa.eu/commission/presscorner/detail/en/ip_15_4956.

European Commission. "Managing Migration Responsibly." Accessed September 11, 2024. https://commission.europa.eu/strategy-and-policy/priorities-2019-2024/story-von-der-leyen-commission/managing-migration-responsibly_en.

European Commission. "Managing Migration Responsibly." Accessed September 11, 2024. https://commission.europa.eu/strategy-and-policy/priorities-2019-2024/story-von-der-leyen-commission/managing-migration-responsibly_en.

European Union. *A European Agenda on Migration*, Communication from the Commission, COM (2015) 0240.

Europol. "Europol's Most Noteworthy Operations." Accessed December 16, 2024. https://www.europol.europa.eu/about-europol/europol-20-years/europols-20-most-noteworthy-operations.

Europol. "Strategic Agreements." Accessed November 24, 2024. https://www.europol.europa.eu/partners-agreements/strategic-agreements.

Financial Action Task Force (FATF). Accessed September 11, 2024. https://www.fatf-gafi.org/.

GAN Integrity. "We Are GAN Integrity." Accessed November 24, 2024. https://www.ganintegrity.com/about/.

Global Initiative Against Transnational Organized Crime. "UNTOC Review Mechanism." Accessed November 24, 2024. https://globalinitiative.net/analysis/untoc-review-mechanism-one-year-to-go/.

Green Customs. "The Green Customs Initiative." Accessed November 24, 2024. https://www.greencustoms.org/.

HTCourts.org. "9 Ways Human Traffickers Recruit Their Victims." Accessed December 16, 2024. https://htcourts.org/ways-human-traffickers-recruit-victims/.

INHOPE. "Somos una red mundial de 54 líneas de emergencia." Accessed September 25, 2024. https://www.inhope.org/EN.

International Action Network on Small Arms (IANSA). Accessed September 11, 2024. https://iansa.org/.

International Action Network on Small Arms. Accessed September 11, 2024. https://iansa.org/.

International Atomic Energy Agency. Accessed November 24, 2024. https://www.iaea.org/.

International Civil Aviation Organization. "Safe Skies, Sustainable Future." Accessed September 11, 2024. https://www.icao.int/Pages/default.aspx.

International Energy Agency. "Energy Technology Perspectives 2024 Out Now." Accessed November 29, 2024. https://www.iea.org/.

International Maritime Organization. "IMO Secretary-General Visits Red Sea Countries." Accessed September 11, 2024. https://www.imo.org/.

International Telecommunication Union (ITU). "Committed to Connecting the World." Accessed November 24, 2024. https://www.itu.int/es/Pages/default.aspx.

Internet Watch Foundation. "Report Online Child Sexual Abuse." Accessed November 11, 2024. https://www.iwf.org.uk/.

Interpol. "5th Interpol Global Conference on Trafficking in Human Beings and Smuggling of Migrants." Accessed November 24, 2024. https://www.interpol.int/fr/Actualites-et-evenements/Evenements/2017/5th-INTERPOL-Global-Conference-on-Trafficking-in-Human-Beings-and-Smuggling-of-Migrants.

Interpol. "Human Trafficking and Migrant Smuggling." Accessed December 10, 2024. https://www.interpol.int/Crimes/Human-trafficking-and-migrant-smuggling.

Interpol. "Information on Interpol Member Countries." Accessed November 24, 2024. https://www.interpol.int/Who-we-are/Member-countries.

Interpol. "Key Dates." Accessed November 24, 2024. https://www.interpol.int/Who-we-are/Our-history/Key-dates.

Interpol. "Resources and Documentation." Accessed November 14, 2024. https://www.interpol.int/Resources/Documents.

Interpol. "Shaping a Global Response to Corruption." Accessed November 24, 2024. https://www.interpol.int/News-and-Events/News/2019/Shaping-a-global-response-to-corruption.

Marini, M., and R. Figueredo. "Brazil's General Data Protection Law (LGPD): What You Need to Know." *Privacy International* (2019).

Merriam-Webster.com Dictionary. s.v. "biohacking." Accessed November 24, 2024. https://www.merriam-webster.com/dictionary/biohacking.

Naif Arab University for Security Sciences. "NAUSS Signs a Memorandum of Understanding with the United Nations Counter-Terrorism Center (UNCCT)." Accessed November 24, 2024. https://nauss.edu.sa/en-us/news/Pages/2-10-2021.aspx.

OECD. "Responsible Business Conduct." Accessed November 24, 2024. https://www.oecd.org/corporate/mne/.

Open Insulin Foundation. "Open Insulin Foundation." Accessed November 24, 2024. https://openinsulin.org/.

Organization of American States (OAS). "Who We Are." Accessed November 24, 2024. https://www.oas.org/en/about/who_we_are.asp.

Organization of Islamic Cooperation (OIC). "The Collective Voice of the Muslim World." Accessed December 16, 2024. https://www.oic-oci.org/.

Oxford University Press. *Oxford Dictionary of Law*. Accessed November 24, 2024.https://www.oxfordreference.com/display/10.1093/acref/9780199551248.001.0001/acref-9780199551248-e-3951.

RAND Corporation. "About RAND." Accessed November 14, 2024. https://www.rand.org/about.html.

Reuters. "European Banks Join Drive to Combat Human Trafficking Using Data." Accessed November 7, 2024. https://www.reuters.com/article/world/european-banks-join-drive-to-combat-human-trafficking-using-data-idUSKBN0OP1RM/.

Small Arms Survey. "Russia's War: Weighing the Human Cost in Ukraine." Accessed September 11, 2024. https://www.smallarmssurvey.org/taxonomy/term/182.

South Asian Association for Regional Cooperation (SAARC). Accessed September 30, 2024. https://saarc-sec.org/.

The Medical Futurist. "The Current State and Future of Biohacking." 2024. Accessed November 24, 2024. https://medicalfuturist.com/the-current-state-and-future-of-biohacking/.

U4 Anti-Corruption Resource Centre. "About Us." Accessed November 30, 2024. https://www.u4.no/.

United Nations Environment Programme (UNEP). "Who We Are, Where We Work, What We Do." Accessed November 24, 2024. https://www.unep.org/.

United Nations Office on Drugs and Crime "Module 7: Models of Organized Criminal Groups." Accessed December 11, 2023. https://www.unodc.org/e4j/en/organized-crime/module-7/key-issues/groups-vs-activities.html.

United Nations Office on Drugs and Crime "Trafficking in Persons and Smuggling of Migrants." Accessed December 11, 2023. https://www.unodc.org/e4j/en/organized-crime/module-3/key-issues/trafficking-in-persons.html.

United Nations Office on Drugs and Crime (UNODC). "Sharing Electronic Resources and Laws on Crime (SHERLOC)." Accessed November 24, 2024. https://sherloc.unodc.org/cld/en/st/home.html.

United Nations Office on Drugs and Crime. "Conference of the Parties to the United Nations Convention Against Transnational Organized Crime." Accessed March 23, 2021. https://www.unodc.org/unodc/en/treaties/CTOC/resolutions-and-decisions-conference-of-the-parties-to-the-united-nations-convention-against-transnational-organized-crime.html#COP5.

United Nations Office on Drugs and Crime. "Director-General of the United Nations Office at Vienna and Executive Director of the UN Office on Drugs and Crime Takes Office." Accessed November 3, 2024. https://www.unodc.org/lpo-brazil/en/frontpage/2020/02/director-general-of-the-united-nations-office-at-vienna-and-executive-director-of-the-un-office-on-drugs-and-crime-takes-office.html.

United Nations Office on Drugs and Crime. "Human Trafficking: Organized Crime and the Multibillion Dollar Sale of People." Accessed November 29, 2024. https://www.unodc.org/unodc/en/frontpage/2012/July/human-trafficking_-organized-crime-and-the-multibillion-dollar-sale-of-people.html.

United Nations Office on Drugs and Crime. "Information on the United Nations Convention Against Transnational Organized Crime." Accessed November 24, 2024. https://www.unodc.org/unodc/en/organized-crime/intro/UNTOC.html.

United Nations Office on Drugs and Crime. "Terrorism Prevention Branch." Accessed December 9, 2024. https://www.unodc.org/unodc/en/terrorism/index.html.

United Nations Office on Drugs and Crime. *Transnational Crime: Let's Put Them Out of Business*. Accessed December 11, 2023. https://www.unodc.org/toc/en/crimes/human-trafficking.html.

United Nations. "Terrorism Prevention Branch." Accessed September 30, 2024. https://www.unodc.org/unodc/en/terrorism/aboutus.html.

United Nations. "UN Global Counter-Terrorism Strategy." Accessed December 12, 2024. https://www.un.org/counterterrorism/un-global-counter-terrorism-strategy.

United Nations. "United Nations Treaty Collection." Accessed November 24, 2024. https://treaties.un.org/pages/ViewDetails.aspx?src=TREATY&mtdsg_no=XVIII-12-a&chapter=18&clang=_en.

United Nations. "United Nations Treaty Collection." Accessed November 24, 2024. https://treaties.un.org/pages/ViewDetails.aspx?src=TREATY&mtdsg_no=XVIII-12-b&chapter=18.

United Nations. "United Nations Treaty Collection." Accessed November 24, 2024. https://treaties.un.org/Pages/ViewDetails.aspx?src=TREATY&mtdsg_no=XVIII-12-c&chapter=18&clang=_en.

United Nations. *UN Treaty Collection*. Accessed September 27, 2024. https://treaties.un.org/Pages/CTCTreaties.aspx?id=6&subid=A.

Viterbi Conversations in Ethics. "Biohacking: The Ethical Implications of Democratizing Biotechnology." Accessed November 24, 2024. https://vce.usc.edu/volume-5-issue-2/biohacking-the-ethical-implications-of-democratizing-biotechnology/.

World Bank Group. "Worldwide Governance Indicators." Accessed November 24, 2024. https://www.worldbank.org/en/publication/worldwide-governance-indicators.

World Customs Organization. Accessed November 24, 2024. https://www.wcoomd.org/.

World Economic Forum. "Our Mission." Accessed November 24, 2024. https://www.weforum.org/.

About the Authors

Anis H. Bajrektarevic, PhD
Professor and Chairperson International Law & Global Political Studies, Vienna, Austria

Anis H. Bajrektarevic is chairperson and professor in international law and global political studies, Vienna, Austria. He has authored nine books (for American and European publishers) and numerous articles on, mainly, geopolitics energy and technology. He is an editor of the NY-based GHIR (Geopolitics, History and International Relations) journal, and editorial board member of several similar specialized magazines on three continents. His 10th book, "Justice and Home Affairs Diplomacy" is scheduled for release later this year in New York.

Carlos López-Veraza Pérez
Public Prosecutor, Alicante, Spain, PhD Candidate in International Law, Carlos III University, Madrid, Spain

Carlos López-Veraza Pérez is Spanish Public Prosecutor with over 13 years of experience, specialized in criminal and civil international cooperation, migrant smuggling, human trafficking, and the legal protection of persons with disabilities. He holds a Master's degree in EU Law and Fundamental Rights and is currently a PhD candidate at Carlos III University, working on a thesis in international criminal law. He is also the author of several legal articles and the book, "Criminal Law in the EU and the Right to a Fair Trial."

Index

O

P

R

S

T

U

W